Reason, Ego & the Right-Minded Teamwork Myth

The Philosophy & Process
for Creating a Right-Minded Team
That Works Together as One

Do No Harm.
Work As One.

By
Dan Hogan
Certified Master Facilitator

Copyright © 2021, 2025 by Dan Hogan, Lord & Hogan LLC. All rights reserved.

Contact Dan Hogan at Dan.Hogan@RightMindedTeamwork.com

This book is licensed for personal, non-commercial use only. No part of this publication may be reproduced, distributed, or transmitted in any form or by any means, including photocopying, recording, or other electronic or mechanical methods, without the prior written permission of the publisher, except for brief quotations embodied in critical reviews and certain other noncommercial uses permitted by copyright law.

ISBN: 978-1-939585-04-2

Acknowledgments & Appreciations

To the thousands of teammates, team leaders, and
team-building facilitators with whom
I've worked with over the last 40 years,

Thank You

For being my teacher.

Collectively, we created this awesome, team-building program.

Right-Minded Teamwork is a business-oriented,
psychological approach to team building where
acceptance, forgiveness, and adjustment
are teammate characteristics,
and customer satisfaction
is the team's result.

In addition, there are several special people I want to joyfully acknowledge and thank for their contributions.

First and foremost, I want to convey my deep and heartfelt gratitude to our editor, Erin Leigh. Thanks to her superb editing and vital guidance, Right-Minded Teamwork is now much easier to understand and successfully integrate in your team. Thank you, Erin. The RMT book series would not have happened without you.
(To contact Erin, email erin@thechoice.life.)

Next, a giant thank you to the Ebook Launch team. Dane Low, our book cover designer, created exceptional cover designs for the Right-Minded Teamwork book series. Thank you for elevating Right-Minded Teamwork. (To reach Dane visit EbookLaunch.com.)

Another sincere thank you goes out to Cathi Bosco, our graphic artist, who renovated and modernized many of our Right-Minded Teamwork process models, graphics, and illustrations.
(reach her at CathiBosco.com).
And I also want to thank the Media A-Team, who created the original and current versions of the Right Choice Model.
(find them at Mediaateam.com).

Finally, I want to express my gratitude to Jackie D'Elia, our website and UX designer, who successfully modernized the RightMindedTeamwork.com website into an easy-to-use platform. Her work allows us to share the RMT books, models, and other resources and materials with the world. Thank you, Jackie.
(Contact Jackie at JackieDElia.com.)

CONTENTS

Preface 11
Right-Minded Teamwork: A High-Level View 21

The RMT Myth 25
   A Message from Reason 25
   The Myth 28
   Moral of the Story 33

The RMT Process 43
   An Overview of the Seven RMT Methods 45
   How to Study & Apply These Methods 50

The Seven RMT Team-Building Methods 53
   Right-Minded Teamwork in Any Team 53
   How to Facilitate Team Work Agreements 81
   How to Apply the Right Choice Model 91
   7 Mindfulness Training Lessons 107
   Right-Minded Teamwork: 9 Right Choices 115
   Design a Right-Minded, Team-Building Workshop 123
   Achieve Your Organization's Strategic Plan 132

The End. Your New Beginning. 140

Glossary of Right-Minded Teamwork Terms & Resources 143
    A Course in Miracles 143
    Accept, Forgive, Adjust 144
    Ally or Adversary Teammate 145
    Avoidance Behavior 146
    Battleground: Where People Are Punished for Mistakes 146
    Certified Master Facilitator (CMF) 148
    Classroom: Where People Learn from Mistakes 148
    Communication Work Agreement 149
    Create, Promote, Allow 150
    Critical Few: Complete Important Tasks First 150
    Decision-Maker: The Real You 151
    Decision-Maker: Trust Your Intuition 152
    Decision-Making Work Agreement 152
    Desire & Willingness: Preconditions for Accountability 153
    Do No Harm. Work as One. ® 154
    Ego & Ego Attack 154
    Moment of Reason 155
    Onboarding New Teammates 156
    Oneness vs. Separateness 156
    Psychological Goals 157
    Reason 158
    Recognition: Make It Easy to Keep Going 159
    Right Choice Model 160
    Right-Minded Teamwork ® Attitudes & Behaviors 161
    Right-Mindedness vs. Wrong-Mindedness 161
    Thought System 162
    Train Your Mind 163
    Unified Circle of Right-Minded Thinking 164
    Work Agreements 165
About the Author 166

Preface

Welcome to Right-Minded Teamwork ® (RMT).

What is RMT?

Right-Minded Teamwork is an intelligent and empowering teamwork system that creates a *team that works together as one*.

Every one of us has the right to experience the magic that can happen when teammates work together as *one unified team*. Each of us can claim and exercise that right, starting right now, if we choose. That is why RMT is for everyone, everywhere, forever. And, through these pages, it is available to you.

Apply RMT, and you will improve your work processes and strengthen your relationships.

Apply RMT, and your team will achieve 100% customer satisfaction.

Apply RMT, and your team will *work together as one*.

You'll also do your part to make the world a better place for everyone, everywhere, forever.

Let's get started right now.

It is an honor to introduce you to this unique, real-world, continuous improvement method. RMT has already improved the lives and teams of thousands of people worldwide. Apply this process in your team, and you, too, will reap its benefits.

Before we get started, you may be wondering if you're in the right place. Is this book for you? What should you expect to learn? Why is this methodology worth considering? Let's go ahead and answer these questions right now.

Is this book for you?

This book is primarily intended as a resource for leaders and facilitators. But it is also much more than that. The content you will find here can positively benefit everyone, everywhere, on any team. RMT is a universal, self-evident, self-validating process with the power to transform even the most challenged team.

What is this book about?

In these pages, we will explore two significant concepts:

- The RMT Myth, a short tale that presents RMT's underlying teamwork **philosophy** of oneness and
- The RMT team-building **process** that helps achieve oneness

The RMT Myth is a short, simple story.

It follows three characters: Reason, Ego, and you, the Decision-Maker. The myth illustrates the Right-Minded Teamwork philosophy, sort of like an aspirational thought system.

Right-Minded Teammates Follow Reason

Simply put, the RMT Myth advocates for teammates to follow Reason's path to oneness and shared interest instead of following Ego's disastrous advice to seek separateness and prioritize selfishness.

In other words, the Right-Minded Teamwork Myth illustrates what "right-minded" thinking and behaving ideally look and feel like.

Once you have read and understood the RMT Myth, you and your team are ready for the Right-Minded Teamwork process.

Unlike the story about Reason, Ego, and the Decision-Maker, the RMT process is no myth. It is practical, deliberate, and reliable.

The RMT process is a set of interconnected, team-building methods that together form a self-perpetuating, continuous improvement system. It allows you to *integrate the aspirations of the RMT Myth into your team in a way that helps you achieve your business goals.*

This book will teach you the RMT process, including seven of RMT's proven team-building methods that lead to continuous improvement.

Why Consider RMT?

There are many common "team-building" practices out there. Three common team-building avenues include: education, games, and social events.

As far as real team building goes, none of these approaches is effective. Not one of them produces proven reliable results. If you have participated in them, you know what I mean.

Still, many well-meaning team leaders continue to use these ineffective tactics, trying to make them work. Usually, this is because they do not realize there is a better way.

Real-World Team Building

A **real-world approach** to team building *is the better way*. It is also the most reliable way to achieve and sustain high-performance teamwork.

Right-Minded Teamwork is a real-world, team-building process.

Applied intentionally, it has the power to transform your team, bringing you together to work as one, and allow you to achieve - or even exceed! - your goals.

Where did RMT come from?

This proven methodology came from people just like you.

Throughout my 40-year career in team building and facilitation, I had the honor of working with hundreds of teams and thousands of beautifully diverse people all around the world. As much as I was hired to help them, they also taught me, every time.

I also like to believe these lessons and methods are universal and have been available to all of us since the beginning of time.

Together, we uncovered the core methods and process of Right-Minded Teamwork. Our collective wisdom revealed them.

Over the years, I strived to capture, distill, and teach these RMT concepts and practices, refining the model over time. Today, it is as clear as it has ever been - and easier than ever for you to understand and apply the RMT framework with your team.

As I often said to those beautiful people over the last 40 years, *"You were my teacher. Collectively, we created this team-building program, a process we eventually named Right-Minded Teamwork."*

Now, you get to reap the rewards, too.

What makes RMT unique?

In my entire team-building career, I've never seen another real-world team-building process like RMT. (And I've looked, I promise).

There are a few practices out there that hold some similarities. They are terrific processes, and they can be helpful in certain circumstances. They can be excellent tools to have in your toolbox. But these practices are built to stand alone, not to function as an integral part of your team.

Right-Minded Teamwork is intended to be applied *within* your team to support you and grow with you.

To clarify RMT's uniqueness, think for a moment about what you really want for your team. I'm guessing it includes:
- a proven, reliable, easy-to-follow approach to continuous improvement
- a way to consistently resolve real issues to sustain high-performance teamwork

No, I'm not reading your mind. I've simply worked with a lot of conscientious leaders and facilitators who, like you, wanted the best for their teams and weren't quite sure how to get there. Fortunately, with RMT, you can have both.

With RMT, you are giving your team a reliable way to resolve issues, sustain high-performance teamwork, and achieve customer satisfaction. RMT will improve your teammate relationships as well as your team's work processes, giving your team everything you need to come together and work as one.

How does RMT address team issues?

What happens when you and your teammates address your issues in a Right-Minded Teamwork way?

When difficult team situations occur, you and your teammates consistently **accept**, **forgive**, and **adjust** your collective attitudes and behaviors. This real-time adjustment allows you to successfully respond and recover from those challenging situations. By resolving the underlying problems, you pave the way for productive teamwork.

Doing so is not always easy, but it really is that simple.

In the following pages, I will introduce you to the *Right Choice Model* and *7 Mindfulness Training Lessons* that explore Right-Minded Teamwork Thinking. These mindfulness methods will guide you and your team towards achieving this highly desirable, emotionally mature approach.

You will know you have magnificently adopted Right-Minded attitudes and behaviors when the Right-Minded Teamwork motto of "Do no harm and work as one" comes easily to your team.

Along the way, you will most certainly create lasting trust, respect, and admiration among yourselves as well as between you and your team's customers.

This is the beauty of real-world team building. It unites teammates in achieving common goals.

Your team's act of uniting is your declaration of interdependence. It is your collective **moment of Reason** and your return to what we call the forgiving Unified Circle of Right-Minded Thinking.

When you join this Circle, you also join others who hold these mindful truths to be self-evident. Moreover, within this Circle, you know that all minds are created equal.

> *Whosoever believes in the oneness of equal minds will, undoubtedly, have everlasting freedom to always choose Right-Minded Teamwork.*

Most importantly, with Right-Minded Teamwork, you will actually resolve your team's problems.

. . . . .

One last thing before closing. Please accept your new special role.

Welcome to Your New Role: RMT Teacher

Now that you have a clearer sense of the journey we'll be taking together through these pages, I want to take a moment to congratulate you on your new role. Incorporating Right-Minded Teamwork into your team-building repertoire means **you are now a Right-Minded Teamwork Teacher.**

As an RMT Teacher, **your specialty is team transformations**.

Using RMT, you help to transform dysfunctional souls into healthy and functional teammates. You guide teammates to convert their mistakes into Right-Minded attitudes and behaviors. They express their deep and heartfelt gratitude for your facilitation efforts and results. Some even say you "saved them."

Whether you're new or experienced in advocating for better teamwork, add RMT to your practice today. There's no reason not to:

All parts of Right-Minded Teamwork are available for your use. There are no licensing or certification requirements.

My only request is that you accept Reason's wisdom on this path. With Reason's guidance, you can easily apply these methods to help your teams create and sustain Right-Minded Teamwork.

My Special Support Function

It took countless workshops, a 35-year career in active team-building facilitation, and the collective wisdom of so many teammates and team leaders to conceptualize and build Right-Minded Teamwork into the robust model it is today.

Though I no longer facilitate actively, choosing to pass that torch on to the next generation of facilitators and teachers, I will always continue to promote Right-Minded Teamwork.

The reason for my continued passion is quite simple. I know, beyond a shadow of a doubt, that RMT is right for every team, everywhere, forever. If you use RMT, it *will* help make your team and the world a better place.

To make that happen, though, **your teammates need you to teach them the Right-Minded Teamwork way.**

As you lead them down the RMT path, remember: I am here to support you. So, reach out to me. Ask me questions. Let me get to know you so I can refer you to clients who are looking for RMT support.

Also remember that even though you will undoubtedly help your teams achieve an "early win," creating and sustaining Right-Minded Teamwork takes at least a year.

So, as you enter into the team-building process, stick with it for the long haul. Plan to stay with your team for at least one to two years. Help them firmly establish RMT in their team. Give them the foundation they need to learn, grow, and succeed.

As you do, you will do your part to make the world a better place for everyone, everywhere, forever.

Let's get started now.

Dan Hogan

Right-Minded Teamwork: A High-Level View

Before we dive deep into the details, let's first take a high-level look at the two parts of the Right-Minded Teamwork model:

The **Myth** and the **Process**.

The RMT Myth

The Right-Minded Teamwork Myth is a story that illustrates how teamwork originally functioned perfectly… and how it deteriorated to where it often is today.

The Myth teaches a "right-minded" philosophy of oneness. It also offers "right-minded" team values, which for the vast majority of teams are not entirely possible to achieve. However, embracing and working towards these idyllic attitudes and work behaviors every day is certainly possible. Doing so is also practical; the Right-Minded Teamwork process will help you get there.

The Right-Minded philosophy, as shown in the RMT Myth, is founded on two universal truths.

None of us is as smart as all of us.

>Right-Minded Teammates know that working collaboratively together, in a Right-Minded manner, is the only way to create the kind of teamwork that achieves 100% customer satisfaction.

Do No Harm and Work as One. ®

>As a Right-Minded Teammate, you can be firm, direct, gentle, and compassionate, all at the same time. You do not blame yourself or others for mistakes. You and your teammates are allies, not adversaries.
>
>You consistently **accept**, **forgive**, and **adjust** your attitudes and behaviors to help your team achieve its goals. You seek solutions. You look for ways to improve difficult situations and to sustain high-performance teamwork.
>
>You do not harm, allowing you and your teammates to always work as one.

Together, the RMT philosophy and its continuous improvement process allow teams to accomplish goals while achieving 100% customer satisfaction.

The RMT Process

The Right-Minded Teamwork Process is built on five interlocking teamwork Elements. These 5 Elements form the core framework of Right-Minded Teamwork. With them, you will successfully apply and operate this teamwork system within your team.

The 5 Elements together create a continuous procedure that contains two goals and three teamwork methods. They are implemented over a six-to-12-month period.

The 5 Elements of Right-Minded Teamwork:

1. Team Business Goals
2. Team Psychological Goals
3. Team Work Agreements
4. Team Operating System
5. Right-Minded Teammate Development

NOTE: Every other Right-Minded Teamwork method discussed in this book is linked to the 5 Elements of Right-Minded Teamwork. You will see these five terms throughout each method we discuss.

Once you understand each Element and how all five fit together to form RMT's powerful, continuous improvement system, you will immediately see the benefits of RMT for you, your teammates, and your customers.

What is "Right" in Right-Minded Teamwork?

RMT has nothing to do with right-brain thinking or right-wing viewpoints.

It has everything to do with what your team, together, decides is "right." Your team's choices, identified collectively, define your team's Right-Minded Teamwork.

> *The "right" way is the way you choose is right for your team.*

So, how do you open up a team discussion about what is right or wrong for your team?

- ✓ You learn about Right-Minded Teamwork through this book.
- ✓ You introduce Right-Minded Teamwork to your team.
- ✓ You apply some or all of the tools and exercises offered here.
- ✓ You watch your team come together doing no harm and working as one.

But for right now, all you need to do is continue reading. On the next page, you'll receive a special message from Reason, written just for you.

The RMT Myth

A Message from Reason

Dear Reader,

My name is Reason. We haven't been officially introduced, but I've been your constant supporter for many, many years.

Though you may think of me as an "I," I am not really a separate entity. I live inside of you. I also live inside everyone else, too. For that reason, it is more accurate to say, "We are Reason," collectively.

The story you are about to read will help you understand what I mean by that.

Here's a little preview:

> Once, there was only Reason. Everyone had everything they needed, and everyone was happy with what they had.
>
> But out of nowhere, a tiny, mad idea crept into our collective minds. For just an instant, we began to wonder,
>
> "Is there more to be gained than what we have achieved by working together as one unified team?"
>
> This moment was the **birth of separation**.

> *Fortunately, most of us just kindly laughed off the silly question. But some listened. They began to think separate thoughts. Some had the thought that if they could work alone and take more for themselves, it would make them even happier.*
>
> *Instead of following Reason's advice, they chose to follow Ego (the obvious instigator of such a thought).*
>
> *Because of their choice to break from Reason, teamwork faltered. Choosing to focus only on themselves impacted everyone.*

As you will see in the coming pages, there is more to this story. But even before you read it, allow this excerpt to prepare you. Open your mind to see the true value, importance, and power of *choice* – your choices and the choices of your teammates.

In every situation, every one of us makes a choice to follow either Reason or Ego. The hope, of course, for the sake of your team's success, is that you and your teammates will choose Reason. When you do, you will do no harm, and you will always work as one.

The most beautiful part is that no matter how far you or your teammates may have strayed, by *choosing* to work *with* Reason, you will inevitably find your way back to collaborative, productive teamwork – your pre-separation state.

When following Reason, it is easy for teammates to make Right-Minded choices. It is natural for them to act and behave as a single, unified team, ready to achieve team goals.

This book and the seven Right-Minded Teamwork methods it introduces will teach you how to get there. With these tools, you and your team will create and follow your own Right-Minded thought system. You will develop Right-Minded, effective work processes.

Reader, I want you to know that I, Reason, am available to you anytime and anywhere, forever. When you are ready to collaborate and work together as a cohesive team, I will be there, in your mind, prepared to show you the way. Together, we will make it happen. Then, you and your team will easily live the RMT motto. You will **do no harm** and **work as one**.

Join me on the Right-Minded Teamwork journey. A mindful *inward* journey. One without distance to a goal you want to achieve.

It's your new beginning. Let's start today.

Forever yours,
~ Reason

PS - Don't hesitate to call on me anytime. It only takes a mindful moment. I am always here for you.

The Myth

Once, before we lived in tribes, we all naturally worked together as one.

All our needs were met. There was no sense of want because there was no need. Peace, abundance, and collaboration were normal. Instead of "yours" and "mine," we shared with each other simply and effortlessly.

There was no leader, either, but there was a clear, guiding spirit that emanated from our collective cooperation. We named that shepherding spirit **Reason**. Reason continually and gently reminded us of our caring thoughts and feelings for one another.

With Reason's guidance, there was no fear. There was no doubt as to who and what we were. We were one, always there for one another. We easily worked together. We needed and wanted each other. We had everything we could ask for.

But out of nowhere, a tiny, mad idea crept into our collective minds. For just an instant, we began to wonder,

> *Is there more to be gained than what we have achieved by working together as one unified team?*

This moment was the ***birth of separation***.

Fortunately, most of us just kindly laughed off the silly question. But some listened. They began to think separate thoughts. Some had the thought that if they could work alone and take more for themselves, it would make them even happier.

Then Reason stepped gently into our collective minds and asked,

But how could we have more than everything?

Reason went on to remind us that we had free will. If we wanted, we could follow that foolish little thought. If we did, it would be just like falling asleep and having a bad dream. Fortunately, Reason assured us that if anyone fell asleep, we would not abandon them. All of us would remain here together, as one, to help them wake up.

For most of us, Reason's gentle question and kind words made sense. We decided Reason's advice was right for us. That decision was our first **moment of Reason**. Shifting our focus back to our teamwork, we continued to work together as one.

But not everyone agreed.

One, named "**Ego**," concluded that if they had more than anyone else, it would make them even more special than Reason - or so they thought.

Ego didn't realize that this idea of being different and special was yet another tiny, mad idea. In the world of oneness, everyone is on the same team, working towards the same goals for the same reasons, contributing fully. There is no value in being an outlier, somehow different than the rest. What would that add to the team? Within the Unified Circle of Right-Minded Thinking, we are all one.

Still, Ego persisted, following the mad idea, and seeking their own way until they began to fall asleep, just as Reason had predicted. As Ego's eyes closed, Reason tenderly placed a folded note alongside Ego. On the outside, it read, *"Open when you are ready to wake up."* On the inside, Reason included practical ideas on how to move back into the Unified Circle of Right-Minded Thinking. Eventually, this vital information would help Ego return.

But let's continue with the story. Fast asleep, Ego didn't notice Reason's gesture or note. To the slumbering Ego, the plan was crystal clear: Get more by taking more from others—more of… everything.

So off Ego went, taking more and more. Even though there was enough for everyone, Ego continued to take extra. But soon, Ego ran into a problem: Where to store all the extra stuff so no one would take it back?

Ego decided to leave and find a place to hide the stuff, somewhere no one could see it or steal it.

Proud of having such an excellent plan, Ego struck up a conversation with some others on the way to taking more stuff to hide. Ego bragged about all the really good stuff already stored away and the excellent plan to acquire even more. Ego even claimed to have more than Reason, which of course, was not true. Ego's illusion - *delusion* - made Ego feel special and important.

Regrettably, Ego was able to convince a few others to join in. They wanted Ego's version of specialness, too. Each of them began taking more, just like Ego.

They called their new group a tribe. Reason, and all those still following Reason's attitudes and Right-Minded Thinking, called them the Separated Ones. For a little while, the separated tribe sort of worked... until one day, a tribe member took stuff from another tribe member.

Now there was conflict. Conflict was a new feeling; no one had experienced it before. Other new emotions, like anger, fear, revenge, grievance, and doubt began showing up in the tribe members' minds as well. Everyone agreed these new feelings were awful. They convinced themselves and each other that their only hope of getting rid of those dreadful feelings was to go out and take more stuff. They tried to cover their fear with *more* - which, in truth, never works.

Soon, the tribe member who lost stuff to the other member became incredibly angry and hostile. They couldn't stand it any longer. A new question crept in: How could they protect their stuff?

One more tiny, mad, Ego-driven idea arose in their mind:

I know what I'll do! I'll leave this tribe and start my own tribe.

From that moment on, more and more tribe members began to join and split off, then join and split again, over, and over. Eventually, their wrong-minded choices created the world we live in today: a world filled with adversaries where once there were only allies.

Today, we have thousands of tribes around the globe taking from one another in more physical and psychological ways than we can possibly count. We live in a complex world of duality and chaos. A world of yours and mine. A world where, far too often, people fight over and take each other's stuff.

Most of us who are stuck in wrong-minded thought systems do not even know we are stuck. Fortunately, as napping Egos, we are only asleep in a nightmarish and chaotic dream where every choice leads to greater dysfunction.

We are dreaming of separation, but in reality, we are still one. If we choose, we can still follow Reason. We can begin our journey back to Right-Minded Teamwork and the unified circle of oneness. It's not too late to wake up.

Waking up means first gently accepting the fact that, as long as we view ourselves as our Egos, we are *out of our right minds*.

Once we accept this - our first **moment of Reason** - we will discover Reason's note, apply the sage advice, and gladly embrace Right-Minded attitudes and behaviors.

Moral of the Story

Wake up.

Shift your perspective.

Return to the Unified Circle of Right-Minded Thinking.

No matter what happens, and no matter how real it may feel or appear, Ego's world is a dream. As a team leader, teammate, or team facilitator, **your new purpose** – your special function – is to partner with Reason to awaken your teammates from their negative, adversarial nightmare and show them how to choose Reason, too.

As you do, you will invite them to participate in creating your team's Right-Minded thought system. This set of team beliefs and behaviors will bring all teammates back into collaborative unity, allowing you to work together as one team.

Reason, Ego & You – the Decision-Maker

Three entities within you influence your daily choices as a Right-Minded Teammate. These three are **Ego**, **Reason**, and the **Decision-Maker.**

Ego and Reason are your teachers and guides. The Decision Maker is the part of you that decides who you will listen to and follow.

You, the Decision-Maker, are a student in life's classroom. This classroom takes many forms. Your team is one of them.

As the Decision-Maker, **you always have free will** to follow either Reason or Ego. It is your choice, and only yours.

Because you have free will, you are 100% responsible for what you think and choose to do. Each morning, whether you are conscious of it or not, your Decision-Maker decides what kind of day you will have by choosing which teacher to follow: Ego or Reason.

Ego is a negative influence who believes your team is like a battleground. Ego is continuously talking inside your mind, urgently telling you it's a desperate and dangerous world out there. You hear that people are murderous and out to get you. Ego reminds you that it is everyone else's fault (not yours!) that you are stuck in this constant battle, endlessly suffering within your team.

Ego is a noisy, wrong-minded teacher, telling you to attack and blame. And if you don't listen and follow Ego's thought system and do what you've been told, Ego attacks and blames you for not adhering to their advice.

At work, your Ego sees all your team's challenges and encourages you to respond with attack or blame. Ego sounds like,

> *I can't believe they've all screwed this up. How could you be such an idiot as to stand with them? I said they were out to get you. We should have done our own thing. I told you they were going to blame you for this.*

Reason, on the other hand, follows a different thought system. Reason is quiet, gentle, and kind. Reason is ready to partner with you to show you how to behave in a Right-Minded, collaborative way.

Reason knows you and your teammates will be much better off when you rise above the battleground and work together as a unified team. According to Reason, your team is a wonderful and safe classroom where you re-learn how to live and work as one.

REASON

Reason waits quietly while Ego rants,
causing fear, guilt, and anxiety to mount inside you.

If it gets too painful, you, the Decision-Maker, say to yourself,

There must be a better way! We need better teamwork!

Expressing your genuine desire for change means you are ready for a **moment of Reason**. As you open your mind, looking for a new way, Reason steps in gently. You begin to wake up. You remember the attitudes and behaviors you long ago committed to living before you followed Ego's advice and fell into the dream.

As those Right-Minded attitudes and behaviors return to you, you soon find better ways to work and interact with your teammates. Together, you grow and evolve, making your collective experience and results better for everyone.

Trust Your Intuition as the Decision-Maker

If thinking about Reason and Ego is new to you, it can be helpful to think of Reason as your positive intuition and Ego as your negative, arrogant, and sometimes vindictive intuition.

At different times throughout our lives, we all listen to and follow each of these teachers.

Stop and remember when you had a hunch or a feeling as to what you should do or say in a particular situation. Did you ignore your intuition? Let's say you did not follow your instinct, and it turned out to be a mistake. What did you say to yourself and others?

> *I wish I had trusted my intuition!*

As this memory illustrates, **you already know how to listen and be mindful** of your intuition. It is your natural, pre-separation state of mind. You just need to do it regularly.

If not...

Remember a time when you became angry, agitated, or annoyed with a teammate. Without thinking, you said mean-spirited things. You, too, were saying to yourself, *"My life can't get better until you change."* Accept it. Your negative behavior happened because you did not stop for a **moment of Reason**.

You were literally out of your right mind as you unconsciously turned towards Ego for guidance.

During your reaction, you were mindless as you followed Ego's advice. Then, after a while, once you stepped back and calmed down, you could see your behavior was a mistake - *only* a mistake, to be corrected, not punished. At this moment, you shifted your perspective. You forgave yourself, and you adjusted by apologizing and promising not to behave that way again. You returned to your right mind.

If you are not accustomed to trusting your intuition but would like to do so more, you will need to practice.

> *The key is to* **pause**, **be still**, *and intentionally* **listen** *for your positive intuition - that* **moment of Reason** *- before you react to a situation or event.*

It is that simple. But that does not make it easy, especially at first. It takes mindful practice to *train your mind* to listen for this joyous, intuitive moment. It takes an unwavering commitment to stop yourself continually, gently, and compassionately when you become angry, fearful, agitated, or anxious.

It is not always easy, but it can be done. Many have learned this skill. You can, too. As the Decision-Maker, you always have free will regarding whether you choose to follow Ego or Reason. Even if you've tried before and failed, you can start again today.

Remember that even with steadfast commitment, it will take practice to excel. You will make mistakes. That's okay. Choose Reason again. Choose to follow your Work Agreements again. And again. When you realize you've chosen Ego, apologize, forgive, correct, forget the mistake and move on. The more you practice, the easier it will get.

You will soon find that as you change your mind, you automatically change your behavior. And when you change your behavior, you transform your team into a lovely learning classroom. The more you make an effort to **be in your right mind**, the easier it will become to **stay in your right mind**.

Now, instead of saying, *"I wish I had listened to my intuition,"* you will say,

I'm so glad I turned to Reason and followed my intuition!

Reason's Personal Note to You

Do you remember in the Right-Minded Teamwork Myth when, as Ego was falling asleep, Reason tenderly placed a folded note alongside Ego? On the outside, it read, *"Open when you are ready to wake up."* On the inside were practical ideas on how to move back into the Unified Circle of Right-Minded Thinking.

Now that you are ready to wake up and help your teammates wake up, too, it is time to read what Reason wrote. You unfold the note and read…

We are Reason

Before you listened to Ego and embraced the tiny, mad idea of separation, everyone stood inside the Unified Circle of Right-Minded Thinking. We were One. We were, collectively, Reason.

You know this to be true. Your own experience has taught you this. There have been times, even in your separated life, when all your needs were met. There was no sense of want because you had what you needed. That experience reflects your pre-separation state.

You have also felt, in the past, safe and secure in Reason's way of living and working with your brothers and sisters.

Remember those moments of Reason. Restore your mind to Reason, follow your intuition, shift your perspective, and your Right-Minded behaviors will tenderly flow through you to your teammates.

Of course, to simply say these words means nothing. You must live these words. Then, they will mean everything.

Choose to step inside the Right-Minded circle of unified teamwork and gently and firmly train your mind and heart to remember your pre-separation state. Say to yourself, "I can elect to change all thoughts of separation. Choosing anything but working together as one unified team is nothing but a dream."

This is the truth.

Within your team and within yourself, it must be said, then repeated many times. At first, it will be accepted as partially true with many reservations. Over time, it will be considered seriously, more and more, until it is finally accepted as truth.

Come back!

Stand confidently inside the circle. Draw your teammates back into living Right-Minded Teamwork behaviors. By drawing your teammates back, you strengthen Reason's way of living in this world for your brother, your sister, and yourself.

Now, follow these instructions. Apply the 5 Elements of Right-Minded Teamwork and the 9 Right Choices. Learn the 7 Mindfulness Lessons of Right-Minded Thinking. And begin your journey back to the place of oneness from which you came.

~ Reason

This story, the Right-Minded Teamwork process, the Right-Minded Teamwork Attitudes & Behaviors, and the RMT Choice Model were inspired by *A Course in Miracles*.

The RMT Process

Seven RMT Methods That Work Together as One

Now that you are familiar with the Right-Minded Teamwork Myth, we will review seven interconnected team-building methods that will help your team achieve Right-Minded Teamwork.

Together, these seven RMT methods create a self-perpetuating, continuous improvement, team-building system that will help you accomplish the Right-Minded Teamwork myth's aspirations of oneness and achieve your team's business goals.

Throughout this book, we will take a look at each of these seven RMT methods. By the end of our time together, you will understand how they interweave to help your team work as one.

As we review these tools, please note that RMT is a robust model. It was developed over decades with the help of hundreds of teams and thousands of teammates from around the world. While there is plenty in this book to introduce you to RMT concepts, each of the seven methods and titles you see below is also a standalone book. Together, these books form a series that teaches the complete Right-Minded Teamwork model.

Once you begin applying Right-Minded Teamwork in your team, you will likely want to go deeper, studying each book in greater depth. As you do, consider this first book a reference tool illustrating how all seven titles work together to support the creation of Right-Minded Teamwork.

For now, let's take a brief look at the seven methods to gain an understanding of what they accomplish and how they fit together. Then, we'll talk about how to study and apply them.

An Overview of the Seven RMT Methods

Right-Minded Teamwork in Any Team:
The Ultimate Team-Building Method to Create a Team That Works as One

Description
The RMT framework, consisting of five unique Elements, includes two goals and three methods. These 5 Elements of Right-Minded Teamwork are implemented in your team over a six-to-12-month period.

Though you may always choose to follow your intuition instead, there is a standard, three-workshop implementation plan for applying the 5 Elements in your team. When you complete the third workshop, you will move on to implementing the 90-day, continuous improvement operating plan, which is described in the fourth of the 5 Elements.

Benefit
Your team will establish an efficient, continuous improvement plan that, when nurtured and maintained, will improve teammate relationships, and create and sustain high-performance teamwork.

How to Facilitate Team Work Agreements:
A Practical, 10-Step Process for Building a Right-Minded Team That Works as One

Description
A Work Agreement describes your teammates' collective pledge to transform non-productive, dysfunctional actions into positive and constructive work behavior.

Work Agreements are emotionally mature choices based on collaboration and achieving customer satisfaction. The 10 steps are written primarily for team facilitators; however, leaders and teammates can easily follow them.

Benefit
Abide by these 10 steps, and you will succeed in creating team Work Agreements that will strengthen and sustain your teamwork and improve customer satisfaction.

How to Apply the Right Choice Model:
Create a Right-Minded Team That Works as One

Description
The Right Choice Model is built on the concept that every person has free will. Free will means you are 100% responsible for how you respond to every situation, circumstance, and event that happens.

When difficult situations occur, you either act as an ally, someone who chooses to demonstrate accountable behaviors, or you mindlessly decide to be adversarial, reacting as a victim or victimizer.

The truth of the matter is **you only have two choices**. You are either an ally or an adversary. Right-Minded teammates choose to be allies. Wrong-minded choices lead team members to become adversarial.

Benefit
After learning the five steps of an accountable Right Choice (the "upper loop" in the model, also known as the Unified Circle of Right-Minded Thinking), teammates will be able to consciously choose to respond to team challenges in ways that align with the team's definition of "right," usually as defined in the team's Work Agreements.

7 Mindfulness Training Lessons:
Improve Teammates' Ability to Work as One
with Right-Minded Thinking

Description
The seven mindful lessons of Right-Minded Thinking can be summed up in one sentence with emphasis on three words: Right-Minded Teammates **accept**, **forgive**, and **adjust** their thinking and work behavior.

Accomplishing all three is part of a Right-Minded thought system. When all teammates strive to live all three consistently, the team creates its very own safe, Unified Circle of Right-Minded Thinking.

Benefit
In every circumstance, especially challenging situations, teammates will use these mindfulness lessons to actively apply the team's chosen, Right-Minded way of thinking and behaving, usually as defined in the team's Work Agreements.

Right-Minded Teamwork: *9 Right Choices for Building a Team That Works as One*

Description
This quick read is an excellent primer on Right-Minded Teamwork. It is a terrific way to introduce RMT to teammates.

This book illustrates nine teamwork choices that will bring your team together. These right choices are universal, self-evident, and self-validating. There is no question you want them on your team.

In the book, each right choice is defined, and exercises for applying each are provided.

Benefit
When you apply the nine right choices, your team will have consciously defined a set of right attitudes and behaviors and will have chosen its own Right-Minded "thought system."

Apply these choices, and you will create the "right" way to successfully work together *for your team*.

Design a Right-Minded, Team-Building Workshop: *12 Steps to Create a Team That Works as One*

Description
This book will teach you how to design a practical, real-world, team-building workshop.

The 12 steps are grouped into three phases: Contract, Commence, and Carry on.

Written primarily for team facilitators, team leaders, and teammates can easily follow the steps to design a successful, team-building workshop.

Benefit

Because this method engages teammates in designing the agenda, it virtually guarantees that teammates *cannot wait* to attend the workshop. They *know* that when they meet, they will get real work done in a safe, "no harm" environment.

Achieve Your Organization's Strategic Plan:
Create a Right-Minded Team Management System
to Ensure All Teams Work as One

Description

An enterprise's Team Management System (TMS) aligns teammate attitudes and work behavior to achieve the organization's strategic plan.

Four phases are involved in creating and deploying your customized TMS. Each phase is part of the TMS model and is outlined in the book. The TMS is based on the use of the Right-Minded Teamwork process in every team.

Benefit

With a TMS, every team in the enterprise is aligned with the strategic plan, thus operating with focused clarity. This alignment ensures all teams are pulling the organization in the same direction. Consequently, the enterprise regularly achieves a higher percentage of its strategic goals.

How to Study & Apply These Methods

After carefully examining the descriptions above, you now have a high-level understanding of the seven methods and generally how they fit together.

As for how to study and apply them, as the Decision-Maker, *trust your intuition first*.

As discussed in the Myth, allow Reason to guide you as to which methods will benefit your team the most right now. If you and Reason have made a choice, study those titles first. You can always learn to apply the other methods later.

If you are not sure, you can always follow the suggested study sequence below.

Studied in this order, you will first learn Right-Minded Teamwork's core framework. Then, you will work your way through the other books, each of which supports the application of the 5 Elements in a specific way.

1. ***Right-Minded Teamwork in Any Team***: This book explores the 5 Elements, the core RMT framework.

2. ***How to Facilitate Team Work Agreements***: This book provides an in-depth application for the pivotal third Element of the 5 Elements model.

3. ***How to Apply the Right Choice Model***: This book is a teaching model. It will benefit you in creating the second Element, your team's psychological goals. It will also guide you to identify your team's chosen attitudes and behaviors for your Work Agreements.

4. *7 Mindfulness Training Lessons*: These seven lessons are part of the fifth Element of the RMT framework, Right-Minded Teammate development.

5. *Right-Minded Teamwork*: These nine choices will support you as you create your team's psychological goals, values, and team Work Agreements.

6. *Design a Right-Minded, Team-Building Workshop*: Follow these 12 steps to design effective, transformational, team-building workshops that teammates actually want to attend, and which tangibly help your team grow and improve.

7. *Achieve Your Organization's Strategic Plan*: Apply these four phases to create an enterprise-wide Team Management System that aligns all teammate attitudes and work behaviors to achieve the organization's strategic plan.

Ready to get started? We'll follow this list as we go deeper into these seven RMT methods.

Our first dive will be into **Right-Minded Teamwork in Any Team***: The Ultimate Team-Building Method to Create a Team That Works as One*, where we'll learn about RMT's 5 Elements.

The Seven RMT Team-Building Methods

Right-Minded Teamwork in Any Team

Overview

Right-Minded Teamwork is a business-oriented, psychological approach to team building where acceptance, forgiveness, and adjustment are teammate characteristics, and 100% customer satisfaction is the team's result.

This book and the 5 Element model it teaches convey the core RMT framework. Every other RMT method is linked to this model. This book will help you successfully operate your own version of this powerful team system.

The model is built upon five interlocking teamwork elements, including two goals and three methods. Over the first six to 12 months of your journey with RMT, you will implement these 5 Elements in your team.

To effectively integrate these concepts and tools, you may follow our standard approach of three team-building workshops. Or, you may create your own approach. If you follow the suggested avenue, you will implement the RMT 90-Day operating system after the third workshop to ensure your team creates and sustains RMT.

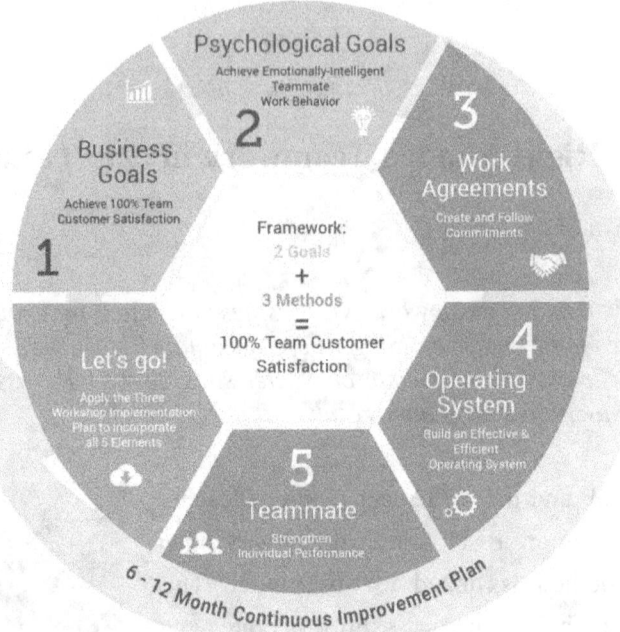

The 5 Elements

1. Team **Business Goals** include your vision, mission, objectives, and customer satisfaction goals and plan.

2. Team **Psychological Goals** are your team's chosen "thought system." They incorporate your team's values, attitudes, and behaviors.

3. Team **Work Agreements** are your team's promises to follow agreed-upon work processes and interpersonal behaviors to help you achieve your business and psychological goals.

4. Your **Team Operating System** is the 90-day, continuous improvement system that ensures you stay focused and on track toward achieving your goals.

5. The **Right-Minded Teammate** is about developing and strengthening teammate skills and abilities to achieve both individual and team goals.

Let's take a closer look at the RMT model and concepts now.

What Is "Right" in Right-Minded Teamwork?

It is worth stating and restating: Right-Minded Teamwork has nothing to do with right-brain thinking or right-wing viewpoints.

> *RMT has everything to do with **what you and your teammates collectively decide is "right."***

Your team's choices on what acceptable work behavior and efficient processes look like define your team's Right-Minded Teamwork "thought system." The "right" way of doing, being, and behaving is the way that is right *for your team*.

The "right" way is how your team decides you will **do no harm** and **work as one**.

So, how do you start the team's discussion about what is right or wrong?

You begin by introducing Right-Minded Teamwork to your team and applying the tools and exercises presented in this book.

Element #1
Business Goal: Achieve 100% Customer Satisfaction

Clear goals focus your team.

For your team to succeed, each team member must first know, understand, and choose to align with the team's overarching performance goals, including the team's vision, mission, and charter.

Said another way, your team is responsible for providing products or services to customers. For the team and the enterprise to succeed, those customers must be satisfied, ideally 100% of the time. It is up to you and your team to identify the processes and behaviors that will get you there - the "right" way for your team. Additionally, teammates must see how their efforts contribute to the team's goals in order to be motivated to help achieve them.

Since 100% customer satisfaction is a nearly universal goal for teams, RMT focuses on guiding teams to achieve this goal.

Within the 5 Elements framework that forms Right-Minded Teamwork, the team's Business Goal is the first Element. This segment of RMT advocates these two tasks:

1. Ask your customers what 100% satisfaction means to them and create a plan to achieve it.
2. Make sure all team business goals align with your organization's strategic plan.

Without clear, aligned goals, team members may falter, become distracted, or fail to fulfill their role on the team. Identifying your Business Goal gets your team on the same page.

Element #2
Psychological Goal: Commit to Your Team's Right-Minded Thinking

Right-Minded Teamwork advocates a psychological approach to team building. Here's why:

> *Your attitudes and thoughts precede and cause your work behavior.*
>
> *Therefore, when you choose Right-Minded thoughts and attitudes, your work behavior also shifts, naturally improving teamwork.*

Commit to Your Team's Right-Minded Thinking

Psychological goals help your team align with your organization's stated values.

To achieve Right-Minded Teamwork, your team must first identify their "right" attitudes. These chosen attitudes form your team's collective, consciously chosen thought system.

Your team's initial Right-Minded Teamwork attitudes are created and agreed upon during the first RMT team-building workshop. Thereafter, they may be adjusted and updated on an as-needed basis.

Your list of "right" attitudes can be short. Here is an example.

We choose these Right-Minded attitudes as our psychological goals:

- *We accept 100% accountability and responsibility for our thoughts and behaviors.*

- *When we make mistakes, we never punish. We do no harm. We work as one. We learn. We recover.*

- *We positively acknowledge and reward each other.*

- *We are we-centered, never self-centered.*

- *When difficult team situations happen, we accept, forgive, and adjust our attitudes and behavior. We always find solutions because we believe that none of us is as smart as all of us.*

- *When new teammates join our team, we will share these goals and ask them to choose them too.*

In that first RMT workshop, teammates work together to choose several psychological goals. Both the agreed-upon attitudes and the team's commitment to living them are captured in team Work Agreements.

Choosing Right Attitudes

To identify "right" attitudes and psychological goals for your team, you have two options:

1. Share the Right-Minded Teammate Attitudes & Behaviors list with the team and allow teammates to choose a few from that list. Or use those ideas to create goals that fit your team better.

   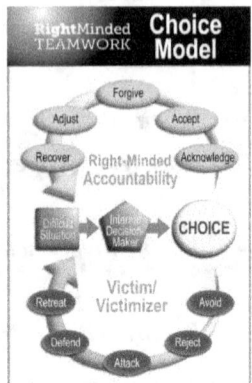

   You will find a partial list of the Attitudes & Behaviors in the *How to Apply the Right Choice Model* section below. For the complete list, see the book ***How to Apply the Right Choice Model***: *Create a Right-Minded Team That Works as One.*

2. Share the Right-Minded Teamwork Choice Model (as described in the *How to Apply the Right Choice Model* book). In a team event, agree on a list of accountable attitudes and work behaviors your team believes are needed to successfully address your teamwork issues and sustain RMT.

   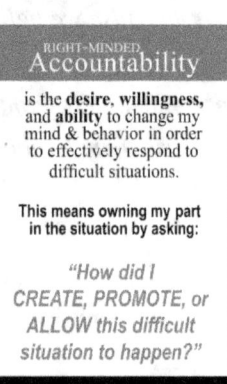

After you create these values and norms for your team, you must commit to living them, usually by capturing them in Work Agreements, the next Element of Right-Minded Teamwork.

Element #3
Work Agreements: Create & Follow Your Commitments

A Work Agreement is a documented, team-building best practice. Work Agreements are one of the most reliable ways to create and sustain a unified team.

A Work Agreement is a covenant, promise, and pledge that transforms dysfunctional behavior into effective work behavior. It is not a flimsy ground rule. It is an emotionally mature promise that, when followed, will create and sustain cohesive teamwork. Simply put, Work Agreements turn adversaries into teammate allies.

Creating and following Work Agreements will:

1. Increase the likelihood that your team will achieve 100% customer satisfaction.
2. Define how the team will align with the organization's business strategy and stated values while pursuing 100% team customer satisfaction.

When followed, Work Agreements ensure your team achieves its psychological and business goals. Work Agreements may also be used to resolve uncertainty, confusion, or conflict around roles, responsibilities, and work processes.

To create Work Agreements, leaders and teammates attend team-building workshops to openly discuss and agree on work performance behaviors that will clear up unresolved interpersonal or work process issues. These challenges are either already hurting the team, or they have the potential to hurt team performance.

Once the team's Right-Minded attitudes are defined, they are documented in team Work Agreements. When teammates align their choices and live their Agreements, their collaboration strengthens the team's ability to achieve customer satisfaction. They work together as one.

Two Types of Work Agreements

Nearly all teamwork issues can be solved with Work Agreements. There are two types of Agreements.

A **process Work Agreement** describes who does what task and which work method they will use to perform that task.

A **behavioral Work Agreement** describes how people will behave while they carry out their tasks.

For complete guidance on establishing effective Work Agreements in your team, see the book ***How to Facilitate Team Work Agreements***: *A Practical, 10-Step Process for Building a Right-Minded Team That Works as One.*

Element #4
Team Operating System: Make Yours Effective & Efficient

A Right-Minded Teamwork Team Operating System is a 90-day, continuous improvement plan that ensures your team stays focused on achieving 100% customer satisfaction.

Your Team Operating System organizes your team processes and procedures. There are six steps in this self-perpetuating process.

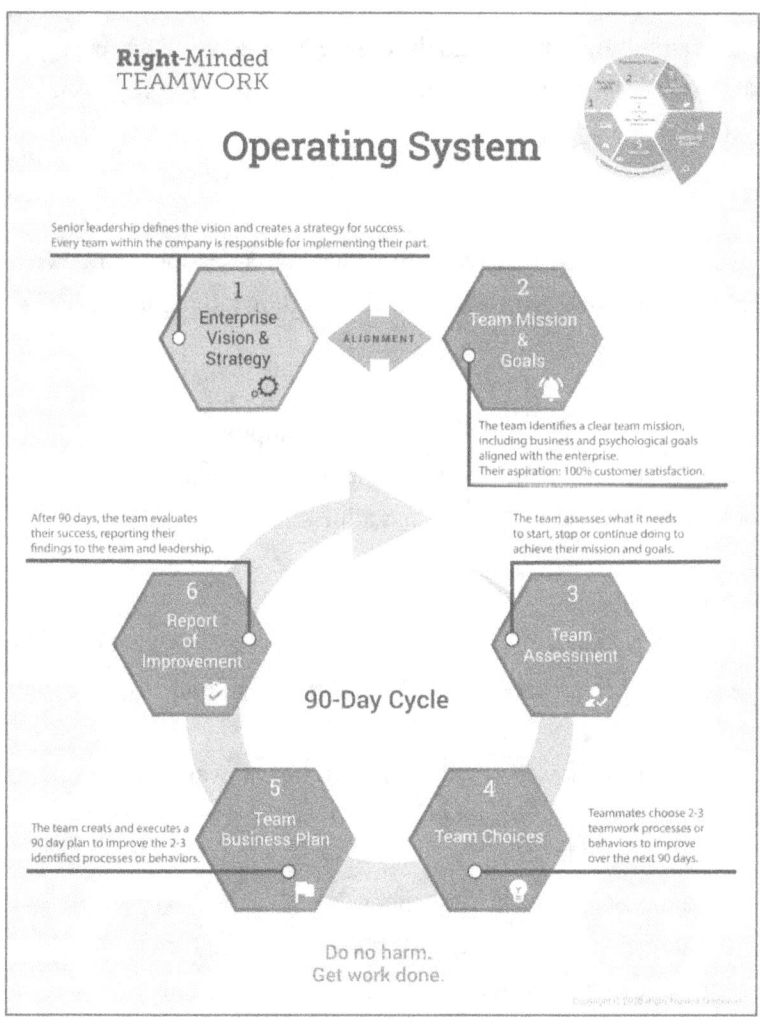

1. Enterprise Vision & Strategy

Your senior leadership team creates a high-level vision and strategy. Every team within the organization is accountable for implementing their part.

2. Team Mission & Goals

Once teammates understand their team's responsibility and accountability to the enterprise's vision and strategy, you create your team's mission, business goals, and psychological goals.

Your team's mission and goals ensure you focus your energy and resources on doing the right things "right" to achieve 100% customer satisfaction.

3. Team Assessment

With clear direction, your team conducts an assessment to determine what your team needs to start, stop, or continue doing to achieve your mission and goals.

The team assessment is used to identify improvement opportunities. To ensure the team stays focused and on track, the team assessment is re-administered every 90 days, and adjustments are made accordingly.

4. Team Choices

In this step, your team identifies one to three critical-few projects, deliverables, or initiatives to achieve over the next 90 days.

You also choose how you will make progress toward those projects or goals using one or more of RMT's three strategies:

- Create process Work Agreements
- Create behavioral Work Agreements
- Implement an improvement project

5. Team Business Plan

All team choices, especially the critical-few projects, are captured in a Team Business Plan. This document is used to guide and track your team's efforts over the first 90 days (and every quarter after that).

6. Report of Improvement

Every 90 days, you conduct another team assessment that calculates actual performance improvement.

A Report of Improvement is created and presented to your team's sponsor or supervisor. You also capture in your report critical lessons learned as well as your best and worst practices.

If your organization has an **RMT Team Management System** [TMS], your quarterly Report of Improvement and lessons learned are given to the TMS Leadership Team for company tabulation and knowledge sharing.

Next, your team leader confirms your team's mission and goals are still aligned with the enterprise's strategic plan. If the team's objectives are still aligned, your team repeats the continuous improvement system by examining team assessment results, identifying opportunities, and taking new improvement actions for the next 90 days.

Element #5
Right-Minded Teammates:
Strengthen Individual Performance

Are you seeking satisfied customers? Do you want to work with collaborative and enjoyable teammates? Do you wish you were part of a team where trust and respect thrive, conflicts are mutually resolved, and teammates support each other in growing their skills and talents?

As a teammate, Right-Minded Teamwork gives you tools to improve your teamwork experience by delivering all these results and more.

Right-Minded Teamwork for Individuals

Working in a Right-Minded team strengthens your ability to be mindful, present, and available for the work at hand.

Rather than waking up each morning in a panic, dreading what the day may bring, you wake up feeling your work is important and valuable. Your contributions matter. Knowing this brings you happiness and joy. Your deep satisfaction helps you enthusiastically greet the day ahead.

When you go to sleep each evening, that feeling of fulfillment calms your mind. You are full of gratitude and honored to work with such incredible people. You are surrounded by teammates who, each day, demonstrate right-minded attitudes and behaviors. RMT allows your team to meet and possibly exceed individual and team goals consistently.

The 10 Characteristics of Right-Minded Teammates

Right-Minded Teammates have many different surface traits and personalities. They are not all alike. They have numerous backgrounds, vastly different experiences, and a wide range of skills.

Nevertheless, it is understood that the Right-Minded Teammate, in their own particular behavioral style, happily lives these characteristics because they align the teammate's authentic *self* with their team's version of the RMT otto: *do no harm, work as one,* and *none of us is as smart as all of us.*

1. Trust	2. Honesty	3. Tolerance
4. Gentleness	5. Joy	6. Defenselessness
7. Generosity	8. Patience	9. Open-Mindedness
	10. Faithfulness	

You will find a complete description of these characteristics in RMT's book: **Right-Minded Teamwork in Any Team:** *The Ultimate Team Building Method to Create a Team That Works as One* and several other RMT books.

Aspiring to Be a Right-Minded Teammate

Every teammate brings two talents to their team: **technical skill** and **personal attitude.**

RMT acknowledges that individuals possess a wide range of technical skills. For example, one teammate could possess strong computer skills while another has exceptional customer service skills. It is not practical to ask the customer service teammate to learn how to fix computers; RMT advocates putting teammates in jobs that best suit their technical skills.

Regardless of their specific roles, Right-Minded Teammates put effort into improving their skills. They also consciously embrace Right-Minded attitudes throughout their workday, focusing their attention on doing the right things the right way, with the right attitude.

When things go wrong, or they realize they are doing the right things the wrong way or with the wrong attitude, Right-Minded Teammates self-adjust their attitude and behavior, usually through a **moment of Reason.**

Combining Technical Skills & Right-Minded Attitudes

One of the best available tools for building teamwork is the book *Right-Minded Teamwork: 9 Right Choices for Building a Team That Works as One.*

Of the nine choices, the seventh choice is:

> *Mistakes happen. Correct them; don't punish people.*

In this choice, when mistakes occur, teammates are asked to trust Reason above Ego. Too often, our instinctual reaction is to criticize, point fingers, or deny responsibility.

> *But if teams are to work as one, the mistake of one is also the mistake of the whole team.*

Rather than blaming the person who made the mistake, Reason encourages you to rise above the battleground to a place in your mind that is strictly solution-focused, not blame-based.

Despite your differences and their inadvertent error, Reason knows you and your teammate have the same goal. The only way forward is to accept what has happened, forgive all involved, and make the necessary adjustments to prevent it from happening again. Focusing on solutions that move you both towards that goal allows you to rise above your differences and work together. Ultimately, this shift helps strengthen individual and team performance.

For example, if a teammate skilled with computers spots a mistake made by a customer service teammate, instead of reacting with anger or blaming the customer service expert, the computer expert could extend an offer to help.

If treated with empathy and understanding, how would the customer service expert respond? Rather than feeling a need to shut down or become defensive, the customer service expert would likely be grateful, if a bit surprised, to receive a genuine offer of support. Together, they could find a way to correct the error and recover.

In this example, the Right-Minded attitude of correcting mistakes and the Right-Minded skill of proper communication brought the situation to an amicable, productive close.

Two Methods for Strengthening Individual Performance

In most cases, it is best to address individual teammate development *after* teammates have participated in the first two RMT team-building workshops (see the Right-Minded Teamwork Three-Workshop Implementation Plan, below). By the time the team has two workshops under their belt, the team's goals and Work Agreements should already be well established. These team goals and Work Agreements inform how and why individual teammates desire to improve their performance, which plays directly into the fifth Element, Right-Minded Teammates.

Once you are ready to focus on improving individual performance within your team, you can:

1. Conduct a Right-Minded Teammate development workshop
2. Implement one-on-one coaching or training

Let's take a brief look at each option.

Conduct a Right-Minded Teammate Development Workshop

To improve team performance, have all teammates participate in a training workshop designed to improve a specific work skill or interpersonal talent.

Examples of work or technical skill development include:
- Boosting team meeting effectiveness through facilitation skills training
- Implementing process improvement training, like Six Sigma
- Using strategic planning exercises, like the Balanced Performance Scorecard
- Improving team problem-solving and decision-making through Kepner Tregoe training

Examples of interpersonal or attitude development include:
- Clarifying teammate roles and responsibilities using RMT's Role Clarification Exercise
- Improving teammate thinking and effectiveness by practicing RMT's 7 Mindfulness Training Lessons
- Learning about teammate characteristics through personality assessment tools - or try the much quicker exercise RMT's About Me & My Preferences Exercise.
- Training teammates how to be assertive (not aggressive or passive) in their communications
- Increasing teammate trust by participating in a Speed of Trust training program or taking part in RMT's Trust Dialogue Exercise

These various RMT exercises can be found in several RMT books, including *Right-Minded Teamwork in Any Team: The Ultimate Team Building Method to Create a Team That Works as One.*

Implement Individual Coaching or Training

When brainstorming development ideas, it's natural for a Right-Minded Teammate to identify individual technical skills or talents they would like to improve.

Examples include:
- Learning a new software program or how to operate a new piece of equipment
- Studying for and obtaining a technical certification
- Attending a management or leadership training program
- Learning negotiation, mediation, or crisis management skills
- Improving the ability to communicate with difficult or angry people effectively

Since most work teams already conduct annual individual performance management assessments, RMT recommends each teammate record at least one personal development goal per year in their performance management program.

An individual development goal might be any of the above examples; however, RMT advocates all Right-Minded teammates to include "developing Right-Minded Thinking" as one of their goals.

Onboarding New Teammates

When a new person, leader, or teammate, joins your team, it is vitally important to properly onboard them within their first week on the job. In a single short meeting where everyone attends, the onboarding is easily and effectively accomplished. Present all your RMT goals and Work Agreements along with why they were created. They ask you clarifying questions. Afterward, you ask them to accept the team's goals and actively live the team's Work Agreements.

Implementation Plan
Three Workshops + 90-Day Operating System

When you are ready to apply the 5 Elements of Right-Minded Teamwork in your team, you have two facilitation options:
1. You can facilitate the process yourself.
2. You can retain a team-building facilitator.

No matter which path you choose, you will want to use RMT's ***Design a Right-Minded, Team-Building Workshop: 12 Steps to Create a Team That Works as One*** to guide you. You will find a brief explanation of this 12-step process later in this section. Following it will greatly increase your likelihood of success.

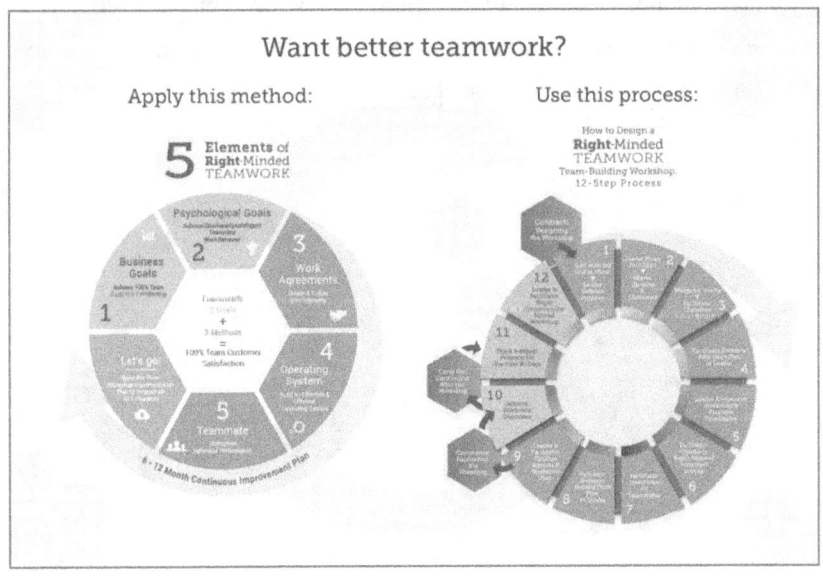

If you choose to hire a team-building facilitator to support you, ask them to follow these steps with you and your teammates.

To find a Certified Master Facilitator, visit the International Institute for Facilitation online at INIFAC.org.

There is no one right way to apply RMT's 5 Elements, but the following plan has worked very well many times before. It will ensure you implement all 5 Elements within your first six to 12 months of deploying Right-Minded Teamwork.

After you complete the initial three workshops described below, your team will transition to the 90-day team operating plan, described in Element #4 above. That 90-day plan will show you how your team will conduct a team workshop every quarter to sustain continuous improvement and achieve team goals.

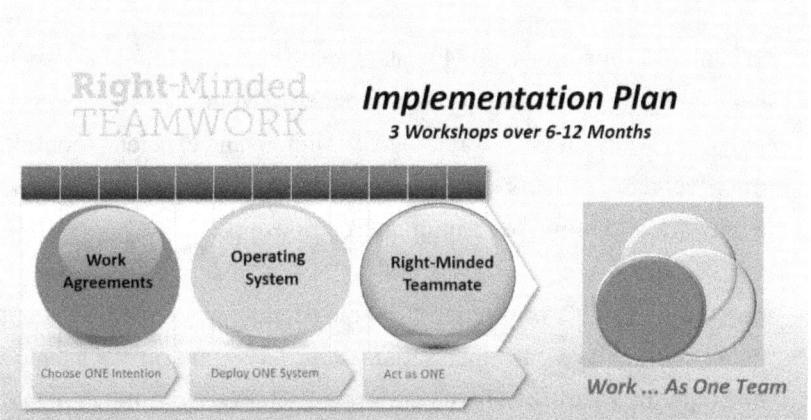

First Workshop – Work Agreements
- Identify team psychological goals and values (Element #2)
- Create at least one team Work Agreement (Element #3)
- Identify 2 or 3 improvement projects for the next 90 days

Second Workshop – Operating System
- Reset and reaffirm business goals (Element #1) and agree on the Team Operating System (Element #4)

Third Workshop - Teammates
- Conduct Right-Minded Teammate (Element #5) development workshop.

90-Day Operating Plan
- Every 90 days, your team meets to assess progress, identify opportunities, take action, and achieve new teamwork improvements.

Benefits of RMT's Three-Workshop Implementation Plan

When you implement RMT as suggested, with three consecutive team-building workshops or in a manner of your choosing, your team will be well on its way to sustaining an efficient continuous improvement process and operating plan for high-performance teamwork and improved teammate relationships.

Most importantly, your team will consistently accomplish its business goals and achieve customer satisfaction. Everyone on your team will be doing their part to help the enterprise achieve its strategic plan.

Benefits of Right-Minded Teamwork

RMT is a real-world method that has profited thousands of people worldwide.

Ultimately, RMT is for everyone, everywhere, forever. It is universal, self-evident, and self-validating.

Praise for Right-Minded Teamwork

A fast read that takes you straight to the root of team dysfunctions and gives you proven, step-by-step tools to improve team function and deliver results. I have paid thousands of dollars for team trainings and workshops that are better summarized here. I am glad to be reminded to choose Reason over Ego and stay in my right mind.
Robin Hensley, *VP IT, UPS*

The author of this guide is all-knowing and has clearly and in a pithy way documented the nine steps to bringing a team together: that togetherness and one-mindedness are key elements to an average team doing extraordinary things. Your work provides a roadmap to use in building a team that works. Again, thank you. I always enjoyed our time together and appreciate all you did for me and my teams.
Alan Kleier, *Former GM/VP, Chevron*

In Right-Minded Teamwork, Dan separates the fun and games of team bonding from the hard work (the muck and mire) of team building. He presents an in-depth model for real-world team building in a realistic, direct, and safe manner. This is a book that you will use and wear out. Right-Minded Teamwork is also a support system, providing a rich array of resources.
Patrick Carmichael, *VP Best Practices Institute, Former Head Talent Management, Saudi Aramco*

What's great about the book is that in addition to the process outlined, the author provides supplemental resources and links to additional information to help you out.
Lauren Bailey, *Maintenance Superintendent, Chevron*

I successfully used the principles of Right-Minded Teamwork in community mediation. I recommend Right-Minded Teamwork to any mediator engaged in dysfunctional behavior in community mediation.
Rick Murray, *JD/Ph.D. Exec. Director, Dispute Resolution Center of the Northwest*

Supportive RMT Methods

Right-Minded Teamwork is a practical, deliberate, and reliable set of interconnected, team-building methods that together form a self-perpetuating process.

In addition to the book ***Right-Minded Teamwork in Any Team****: The Ultimate Team-Building Method to Create a Team That Works as One*, the following supporting texts and tools are encouraged to ensure your team successfully applies and integrates Right-Minded Teamwork and achieves team goals.

How to Facilitate Team Work Agreements*: A Practical, 10-Step Process for Building a Right-Minded Team That Works as One*

Work Agreements are the third of RMT's 5 Element framework. This supporting text explores the power of Work Agreements and teaches you how to create and implement them in your team.

How to Apply the Right Choice Model*: Create a Right-Minded Team That Works as One*

This book is an active teaching model. It will help you and your team identify specific attitudes and behaviors for your Work Agreements.

7 Mindfulness Training Lessons*: Improve Teammates' Ability to Work as One with Right-Minded Thinking*

These seven lessons are integral to Right-Minded Teammates (the fifth Element in RMT's 5 Elements model). If you want Right-Minded Teammates on your team, this book will support their growth and development.

Right-Minded Teamwork*: 9 Right Choices for Building a Team That Works as One*

This short book is a valuable primer that will help teammates embrace Right-Minded Teamwork. It is a good idea to ask teammates to read this book before the first team workshop. These nine choices will also help you create the team's psychological goals, values, and Work Agreements.

Design a Right-Minded, Team-Building Workshop*: 12 Steps to Create a Team That Works as One*

Follow these proven steps to design successful, effective team workshops that teammates actually look forward to attending.

Achieve Your Organization's Strategic Plan*: Create a Right-Minded Team Management System to Ensure All Teams Work as One*

Establishing an enterprise-wide Team Management System [TMS] ensures your organization's ability to employ Right-Minded Teamwork in every team.

How to Facilitate Team Work Agreements

Overview

Work Agreements are the third Element of Right-Minded Teamwork's 5 Elements framework. They are used to transform unproductive, dysfunctional behavior into positive and constructive work behavior.

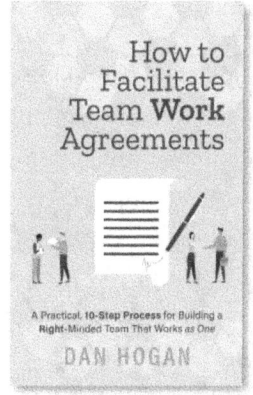

The 10 steps involved in creating Work Agreements are outlined in the book *How to Facilitate Team Work Agreements: A Practical, 10-Step Process for Building a Right-Minded Team That Works as One.*

This book is written primarily for team facilitators, but leaders and teammates can easily follow along to build Work Agreements, too. In this section, we'll take a closer look at this powerful tool for team building.

What Are Work Agreements?

Work Agreements are team covenants or vows that transform teammates' dysfunctional and non-productive behavior into team cohesiveness and accomplishment.

Work Agreements are not guidelines or ground rules. They are emotionally mature promises that guide a team to work collaboratively toward the shared goal of achieving customer satisfaction.

> *If you've ever been part of a team, you know it is not a matter of if conflict will occur among teammates. It is a question of when.*

A team without Work Agreements is like a machine without an operator's manual. Teammates may function at acceptable levels for a while, but eventually, they will decline into separateness and self-interest.

It is far better to have Work Agreements in place before teammate disagreements happen. Established Work Agreements can serve to mitigate and even make positive use of those clashes when they occur. However, even if your team is already in conflict, it's still not too late (and will never be!) to create and live team Work Agreements.

To create Work Agreements, leaders and teammates must openly discuss unresolved interpersonal or work process issues and together agree on what acceptable behavior looks like going forward. Emotionally mature and productive teammates intentionally create Work Agreements because they have experienced the benefits of a unified team with shared interests and common goals.

In my 35 years of active team building, I facilitated over 500 teams around the globe, many of them beautifully diverse and multicultural.

Every single team created Work Agreements and succeeded as a result.

> *Work Agreements work when teammates live them.*

The process for facilitating Work Agreements is not complicated. Nonetheless, becoming proficient in facilitating their creation takes dedication and a willingness to learn. As you practice, you will make mistakes, especially in the beginning. Don't give up. Your mistakes will not hurt your teams - I promise. The long-lasting benefits you will bring to the team as you improve your facilitation skills will far outweigh any initial missteps.

By following the steps in the book ***How to Facilitate Team Work Agreements:*** *A Practical, 10-Step Process for Building a Right-Minded Team That Works as One*, you can learn how to facilitate Work Agreements for your team.

Two Types of Work Agreements

Work Agreements may be process-driven or behavior-driven.

A **process Work Agreement** describes who will do what task and which work method they will use. It defines work tasks in terms of roles, responsibilities, interfaces, or procedures.

A **behavioral Work Agreement** describes how people will behave while performing tasks, such as the ways teammates will bring to light, communicate, and resolve difficult performance issues or teammate conflicts. This type of Work Agreement aims for transparency in all interpersonal interactions.

A Work Agreement that is wholeheartedly agreed upon includes an **intention statement** that defines your team's choice followed by **clarifications or conditions for acceptance**.

Example:

Intention:
Each teammate will communicate their thoughts and feelings in appropriate ways.

Clarifications or Conditions:
- We follow the spirit and intent of our company values.
- If we believe another person is communicating inappropriately, we will call it to their attention in private.
- Even though this Agreement addresses inappropriate communication behaviors, we also agree to give positive teammate reinforcement when we see and hear excellent communication.

Below you will find two real examples. The first one is a behavioral team Communication Work Agreement. The other is a process, Decision-Making Work Agreement.

I worked with these teams for a few years. They were phenomenally successful Agreements because teammates passionately created and actively lived them day in and day out.

Real Team Work Agreements

Behavioral Agreement – Communication

Team Choice: Intention Statement
1. Each teammate will communicate in a respectful way.

Clarifications / Conditions for Acceptance:

A. We will use good communication techniques that include appropriate body language and tone of voice, plus suitable words.
B. If we see or hear disrespect or we hear an inappropriate behind-the-back conversation, we own it and need to step in.
C. If someone unintentionally shows disrespect, we will give them the benefit of the doubt, let them know, and create a new way to interact going forward.
D. We will actively support team decisions in word, deed, and energy; we will use our decision-making protocol agreement for key decisions.
E. We will be on time for meetings.
F. We will ask, "May I interrupt you?"
G. We will use observable facts during disagreements and decision-making, and we will acknowledge when we are using assumptions.
H. We will understand each other's roles, ask for help if we need it, share relevant information and if helpful, give constructive feedback in private.
I. If someone continues to break this agreement, we will tell them that we will invite a third party to help if there is continued disagreement. If that doesn't solve the issues, we will all go to a higher authority for support and resolution.

With my guidance, it took this 10-person team about 4 hours to create these two Work Agreements.

Use your imagination as to what they said to each other that made these successful agreements.

Process Agreement – Decision-Making Protocol
Team Choice: Intention Statement 1. We will go for consensus for all key team decisions, but our fallback will be that Maria [team leader] will decide if we cannot reach a consensus.
Conditions for Acceptance / Clarification A. Before entering a discussion, we'll agree on the decision-making method and fall back, plus when [date] a decision will be made. B. Before delving into a solution, we will create an opportunity or problem statement. C. At the beginning of our discussion, we will determine boundaries & givens (i.e., time sensitivity; cost, hassle, impact, 80% or 100% perfect decision, etc.). D. We provide a business case (appropriate justification) for our decision, including cost/benefit. E. During our conversations, we will advocate and inquire. We will not hold back. For instance, we will acknowledge assumptions and facts. F. To create the best solutions, we will also think about alternative ways to test our solution (Devil's Advocate). G. If we find ourselves at an impasse, we will call a "time out" to calm down or acquire more technical information. H. When a decision is made, we will accurately represent and support the decision. I. We do this Agreement because we want to improve teamwork and trust in one another. J. We will hold ourselves and others accountable for living the letter and the spirit of this Agreement; we will fine-tune it as necessary

Onboarding New Teammates

When a new person, leader, or teammate, joins your team, it is vitally important to properly onboard them within their first week on the job. In a single short meeting where everyone attends, the onboarding is easily and effectively accomplished. Present all your RMT goals and Work Agreements along with why they were created. They ask you clarifying questions. Afterward, you ask them to accept the team's goals and actively live the team's Work Agreements.

Benefits of Team Work Agreements

When created by the team and supported by the team, Work Agreements strengthen and sustain your teamwork, allowing you to achieve team goals and improve customer satisfaction.

Once you have familiarized yourself with this straightforward, practical approach, you will wonder how your team ever functioned without Work Agreements.

Supportive RMT Methods

In addition to the book ***How to Facilitate Team Work Agreements****: A Practical, 10-Step Process for Building a Right-Minded Team That Works as One,* the following supporting texts and tools are encouraged to ensure your team successfully applies and integrates Right-Minded Teamwork and achieves team goals.

Right-Minded Teamwork in Any Team*: The Ultimate Team-Building Method to Create a Team That Works as One*

This book teaches the 5 Elements model, which forms the core RMT framework. To frame the purpose and value of creating team Work Agreements, it can be helpful to briefly introduce RMT's 5 Elements model to the team.

How to Apply the Right Choice Model*: Create a Right-Minded Team That Works as One*

This book is a teaching model. Often, leaders and facilitators present this model to the team at the beginning of the first workshop, before the team creates their first set of Work Agreements. Showcasing this model serves as a way of setting a positive and accountable atmosphere and tone.

7 Mindfulness Training Lessons*: Improve Teammates' Ability to Work as One with Right-Minded Thinking*

These lessons are taught and applied in support of the fifth Element of the 5 Elements model. Right-Minded Teammate development is the suggested topic for the third team-building workshop in RMT's three-workshop implementation plan.

Right-Minded Teamwork: *9 Right Choices for Building a Team That Works as One*

This book is a valuable Right-Minded Teamwork primer that also introduces Work Agreements. Many team leaders and facilitators ask all teammates to read this short book before the first Right-Minded Teamwork workshop.

Design a Right-Minded, Team-Building Workshop: *12 Steps to Create a Team That Works as One*

For a successful and impactful team-building event, follow the 12-step model to design your Work Agreements workshop.

Achieve Your Organization's Strategic Plan: *Create a Right-Minded Team Management System to Ensure All Teams Work as One*

An enterprise-wide Team Management System [TMS] that integrates team Work Agreements throughout all levels and departments leads to improved productivity, happier clients, and greater profits. As a bonus, you'll grow a team of facilitators who can continue to support the organization's success by facilitating future Work Agreements workshops.

How to Apply the Right Choice Model

Overview

Right Choice is a teaching model that promotes Right-Minded, accountable work behavior.

When teammates make wrong-minded choices, they follow Ego into a land of victimization and self-interest.

The Right Choice Model teaches teammates how to wake up from Ego's nightmare and follow Reason into the land of collaboration and ally behavior.

What Is the Right Choice Model?

The Right Choice Model is a tool to help you and your teammates make the conscious choice to follow *your team's* right attitudes and behaviors.

The model, printed on your computer and given to your teammates, is available in a 3x4 inch card and an 8x11 inch poster. It consists of two parts.

The first part contains two loops. The upper loop describes Right-Minded Accountability, and the lower loop defines victimization.

The other part presents the Right-Minded Accountability definition plus the important Right-Minded question that moves you and your teammates back into your right mind.

Right Choice promotes the concept that every person has free will. Free will means you are 100% responsible for how you respond to every situation, circumstance, and event that happens.

When difficult team situations occur, you either:

- Act as an ally, choosing to demonstrate accountable, responsible, and Right-Minded behaviors.

- Choose to be adversarial, reacting to the difficult situation by becoming a victim or victimizer and demonstrating wrong-minded behaviors.

REASON, EGO & THE RIGHT-MINDED TEAMWORK MYTH · 93

Wrong choices lead to victimization, blame, and punishment among teammates. They guarantee solutions are not found because teammates are too busy pointing fingers at others and defending themselves.

Right-Minded choices are the only sane response to challenging team situations. Why? Because teammates who demonstrate the Right actions and behaviors find real solutions to their problems.

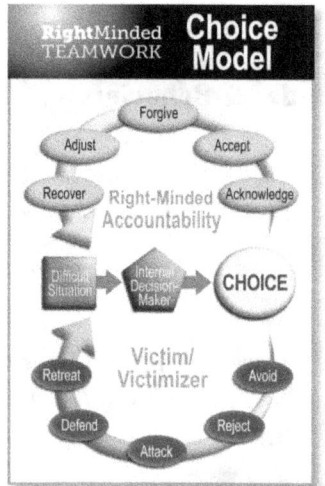 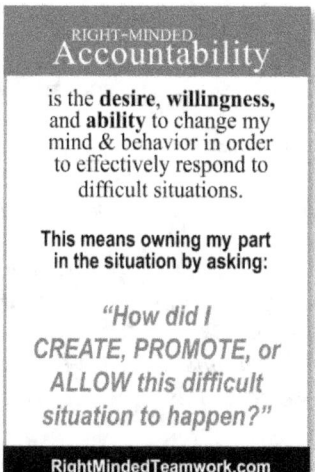

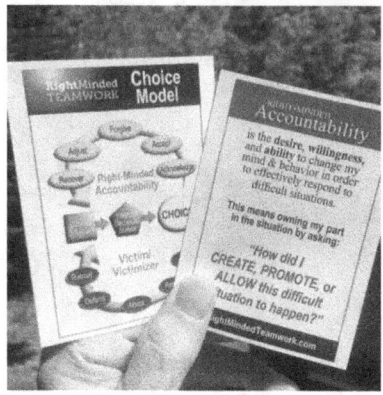

Print and give all teammates the Right Choice Model poster and card.

Who Decides What Is Right?

You and your teammates collectively choose your team's Right attitudes and behaviors.

Below are four examples of Right-Minded Teamwork Attitudes & Behaviors. You will find the full list of over 30 attitudes and behaviors in several RMT books, including ***How to Apply the Right Choice Model****: Create a Right-Minded Team That Works as One*. You can adapt and adopt them for use in your team.

Example RMT Attitudes & Behaviors

We demonstrate contrarian competition and power struggles [Ego], or we demonstrate collaboration and synergy [Reason].

We exhibit victimization behavior [Ego] or we demonstrate accountable and responsible behavior [Reason].

We believe mistakes are bad and obsess over then [Ego] or we choose to believe "we are not our mistakes" and learn from them [Reason].

We embrace and demonstrate forgiveness when mistakes happen [Reason]. We hold grievances or tell ourselves and others that we will never forgive or forget [Ego].

EGO

DECISION MAKER

REASON

You Only Have Two Choices

The Right Choice Model teaches that you only have two choices regarding how you respond to every difficult situation.

Yes – only two.

You can either follow Reason, who teaches Right-Minded attitudes, or you can follow Ego, who teaches victimization and blame. In all team situations, you, the Decision-Maker, choose one or the other.

Please listen carefully: there are many variations of those two choices. Nevertheless, there are still just two.

There is no compromise in this regard.

At all times, you are either mindful, or you are mindless. You are either following Reason or Ego.

You are in your right mind or your wrong mind.

You have free well. The choice is always yours.

Mindfulness Is Choice in Action

When you are mindless, you don't think or reflect. Instead of *consciously* choosing how to respond, you react *unconsciously* in an emotionally immature way, blaming others or avoiding the situation altogether.

When you're mindful, you reflect and carefully choose how you respond to everything that happens to you and around you. When a problematic situation happens, being mindful means asking yourself the question on the Right Choice Model:

How did I **create**, **promote**, *or* **allow** *this to happen?*

Your answers to this question help you and your team experience a **moment of Reason**, which paves the way for you to create real solutions.

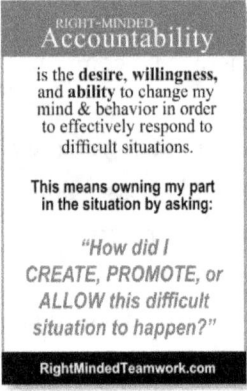

As an example, let's assume a significant mistake has happened in your team.

Half the team is aggressively blaming the other half for the mistake in what is often called an **"Ego attack."** Teammates are making toxic and hurtful statements, directly and indirectly, about each other. The team is stuck in a battleground of "attack and defend." No one is working to resolve the mistake.

REASON, EGO & THE RIGHT-MINDED TEAMWORK MYTH · 97

Seeking a **moment of Reason**, you ask yourself,

*What am I doing to **create**, **promote**, or **allow** this blaming conversation to continue?*

You realize you've been standing by and saying nothing. **You were avoiding**, which is the **first step in the lower loop** of the model.

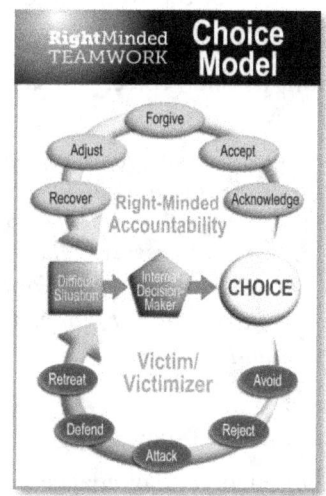

Now that you are aware of your attitude and behavior, you change your mind. You choose to follow Reason and act in a Right-Minded, accountable way, just as your Work Agreement states.

Reason is that part of your mind that always speaks for the Right Choice attitudes and behaviors. When you need a **moment of Reason**, to find the best way to respond to a difficult team situation, say to yourself:

I am here only to be truly helpful.

I am here to represent Reason who sent me.

I do not have to worry about what to say or what to do because Reason who sent me will direct me.

You remember these two Right-Minded aspirations:
- Engage in helpful problem-solving communication.
- Advocate for correcting mistakes rather than punishing others.

As you reflect while holding these two choices in your mind and heart, answers come to your *"right"* mind. In a calm, "do-no-harm-work-as-one" voice, you say,

> *Here's a suggestion. Let's discuss what we know, the facts, about what happened. Then let's find an immediate solution.*
>
> *After we resolve the mistake, let's have a second team discussion to create Work Agreements, not to blame, so that this mistake doesn't happen to our team again. How does that sound?*

If you had followed Ego's advice and continued your avoidance behavior, the conflict would have continued. Since you chose to look towards Reason, you created an environment where you and your teammates **recovered** from the mistake, the **final step in the upper loop** of the model.

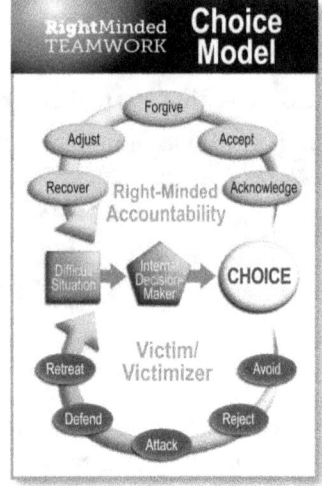

Reason, as always, has brought you - and hopefully everyone else, too - *back into your right mind.*

How do you know you have witnessed a moment of Reason?

You hear a statement like this that relates to a team's Work Agreement:

> "We've already agreed how we were to address that issue, haven't we?"

I heard this **moment of Reason** statement in a team's second RMT workshop. When the team realized they had created Work Agreements three months prior that addressed the issue they were re-arguing, they immediately shifted back into their collective right mind.

To find the full, and short, story go to our book ***How to Facilitate Team Work Agreements***: *A Practical, 10-Step Process for Building a Right-Minded Team That Works as One.*

Look for the section Sustaining Team Work Agreements and find the article titled:

> *"We've already agreed on how we were to address that issue, haven't we?"*

It would be one of the most important lessons you could learn in that book.

How to Apply the Right Choice Model

In the book, you will find a detailed explanation for applying the Right Choice Model in your team. You will also have access to resources, downloads, and videos. For now, here is a brief overview of how to present and apply the Right Choice Model to your team.

Present the Right Choice to teammates.

In a team meeting with all teammates attending, present the Right Choice Model.

Give each teammate a Right Choice Card. You can download them at RightMindedTeamwork.com.

- During the team meeting, compare and contrast Right-Minded, accountable behavior (the upper loop) to wrong-minded, victim behavior (the lower loop).

- Ask the team, "Do we all agree that we want to function as Right-Minded teammates?" Everyone will agree.

Apply Right Choice behaviors to a team challenge.

- All teammates agree to discuss a recent team challenge.

- Teammates ask themselves, *"What did we do or say to **create**, **promote**, or **allow** this team challenge to happen?"*

- Your open and honest discussion leads to potential behavioral or work process solutions. These solutions are captured in team Work Agreements.

You and your teammates live and follow your Work Agreements.

- Following your team meeting and discussion, all teammates do their part to adhere to your Work Agreements.

- When mistakes are made, or someone forgets to apply their Work Agreements, your teammates will actively remind and support each other to get back on track.

- In short, your team follows the Right-Minded Teamwork motto: Do no harm and work as one.

The result: satisfied customers

- When all teammates work together as one unified team, you are able to meet or exceed your customer's expectations.

Benefits of Applying the Right Choice Model

Teammates – Achieve Right-Minded Accountability

After learning the five steps of an accountable choice (the upper loop in the Right Choice Model), teammates will understand and choose to respond to team challenges in a consciously chosen, Right-Minded way, using tools like **moments of Reason** and **Work Agreements** to guide them. The upper loop is also known as your team's Unified Circle of Right-Minded Thinking.

Customers – Achieve 100% Satisfaction

Right Choice also ensures your team will meet and sometimes exceed your customer's expectations.

Let's say one of your **customers is not happy** with the service or the product you are giving them right now. Let's also say your poor or marginal quality has cost them time and money. Specifically, they must wait for their product or have to redo some or much of your work. In other words, **your errors cost them money**, and it is hurting your team's reputation.

The Right Choice model says *you have only two choices* regarding how you will respond to your customers' frustration with your performance. You can either choose to act like a victim or a victimizer, saying it is not your fault and blaming someone else, maybe even the customers themselves.

Alternately, you can choose to follow your team's thought system and behave in a Right-Minded, responsible way.

To make this choice, ask yourself, "What have I/we done to **create, promote,** or **allow** our customers' dissatisfaction?" Your answers will uncover dysfunctional teamwork behaviors.

Instead of punishing your team for their past choices, you correct teamwork behaviors by creating and following Work Agreements that state the Right-Minded way to choose and behave.

When teammates follow their Work Agreements, they will eventually deliver a quality product on time with no rework required. This increases the likelihood of regaining your customers' confidence, trust, and satisfaction. As you continue to meet your customers' expectations, you win as a team, and your customer benefits too.

They benefit. You benefit. Everyone wins.

Supportive RMT Methods

In addition to the book *How to Apply the Right Choice Model*, the following supporting texts and tools are encouraged to ensure your team successfully applies and integrates Right-Minded Teamwork and achieves team goals.

Right-Minded Teamwork in Any Team*: The Ultimate Team-Building Method to Create a Team That Works as One*

Presenting the RMT 5 Elements model as outlined in this book is a valuable way of framing the team's context for applying the Right Choice Model. Specifically, the Right Choice will help the team achieve 100% customer satisfaction (Element #1), create psychological goals (Element #2), and establish team Work Agreements (Element #3).

How to Facilitate Team Work Agreements*: A Practical, 10-Step Process for Building a Right-Minded Team That Works as One*

Your team's collectively agreed-upon Work Agreements, which this book will teach you to create, are essentially behavioral descriptions of your team's Right Choices.

7 Mindfulness Training Lessons*: Improve Teammates' Ability to Work as One with Right-Minded Thinking*

These 7 Lessons are part of Element #5 of the RMT framework, which focuses on Right-Minded Teammate growth and development. The core question of the Right Choice Model ("How did I create, promote, or allow this difficult situation to happen?") is interwoven into the 7 Lessons.

Right-Minded Teamwork*: 9 Right Choices for Building a Team That Works as One*

This book is a valuable Right-Minded Teamwork primer. Many team leaders and facilitators ask all teammates to read this short book before the first Right-Minded Teamwork workshop. The Right Choice model is mentioned in this book and is woven throughout the 9 Right Choices.

Design a Right-Minded, Team-Building Workshop*: 12 Steps to Create a Team That Works as One*

Follow these steps to design your Right-Minded Teamwork workshops. The Right Choice Model is often included in the final workshop agenda.

Achieve Your Organization's Strategic Plan*: Create a Right-Minded Team Management System to Ensure All Teams Work as One*

Right Choice is a universal model that can benefit your entire organization. When you implement an enterprise Team Management System [TMS] that incorporates the Right Choice, everyone is taught how to accept accountability for their behavior and decisions resulting in teams working more cohesively and productively.

7 Mindfulness Training Lessons

Overview

Do you desire a world...

That you rule instead of one that rules you?
Where you are powerful instead of helpless?
In which you have no adversaries, only allies?
Where you and your teammates consistently choose Reason over Ego?

If you answered yes to these questions, the 7 Mindfulness Training Lessons will help you achieve your goals.

These lessons can be summed up in one sentence, with emphasis on three words:

*Right-Minded Teammates **accept**, **forgive**, and **adjust** their thinking and work behavior.*

The 7 Mindfulness Training Lessons

Mindfulness is your conscious ability to monitor your thoughts in the present. When you are mindful, you calmly acknowledge and accept your thoughts, feelings, and behaviors, as well as those of others.

Your calm mindfulness is the necessary condition for receiving a **moment of Reason**, which is a precursor for finding real teamwork solutions.

When you practice mindfulness by following these 7 Lessons, you also practice the Right-Minded attitudes and behaviors taught to you in the Right Choice Model.

The 7 Lessons

1. I am not upset about this difficult situation for the reason I think.

2. I **Accept** and own my part in this situation.

3. It's impossible that my thoughts about this situation are neutral.

4. I **Forgive** others and myself.

5. I will transform the effects of this difficult team situation.

6. I **Adjust** my thinking and behavior.

7. I see every difficult team situation as a learning opportunity.

In every circumstance, and especially during difficult team situations, Right-Minded Teammates use these lessons to practice mindfulness and move them into a Right-Minded, "we are allies" way of thinking and behaving.

These lessons are effective. Apply them, and you, along with Reason's help, will find the best way to respond in all challenging situations and circumstances.

Applying the 7 Lessons: Self-Study or Team Study

There are two options for applying the 7 Mindfulness Lessons:
1. self-study or
2. team study.

Both are recommended.

Be sure to give the 7 Lessons Cards and Posters to your teammates. You can download them at RightMindedTeamwork.com.

If you are pursuing self-study, you will learn how to use the lessons in a difficult situation you likely know very well: the **Constantly Complaining Teammate** (CCT).

Having a Constantly Complaining Teammate on your team may be the reason you are seeking teamwork solutions.

Though a CCT's complaints may look or sound different day to day or from team to team, a similar message usually underpins their efforts. They typically insist,

> *My life can't get better until you change.*

They believe they are right. They think you and everyone else are wrong. That is why they believe you must change.

Fortunately, the challenge of the CCT can be addressed using the 7 Mindfulness Lessons. The book will show you how. Once you understand how to apply these 7 Lessons with a CCT, you will know how to do the same in all your difficult situations.

If you are opting for a team approach, in addition to the *7 Mindfulness Training Lessons* book, you will also want to consult the book **Right-Minded Teamwork in Any Team**: *The Ultimate Team-Building Method to Create a Team That Works as One*.

In that book, you will discover a three-workshop implementation plan. If you choose to follow the plan, the third workshop, focused on Right-Minded Teammate development, is a wonderful time to explore and discuss how the 7 Mindfulness Lessons may be applied in your team.

7 Lessons: A Testimonial

While working on this book series, I received a note from a Right-Minded Teammate who had actively applied the 7 Lessons to transform a challenging situation. She shared:

> *Recently, I was reflecting on a challenging situation with a fellow entrepreneur (not my "team," per se, but within my circle of influence). As I was trying to figure out how I wanted to approach it, the first of the 7 Lessons of Right-Minded Thinking popped into my mind.*
>
> ***"I am not upset about this difficult team situation for the reason I think,"*** *I told myself. Immediately I could see there was more to the situation than just the surface-level issue. No wonder it felt so heavy and complicated.*
>
> *Seeing as I'd already made progress, I figured I might as well apply the next few Mindfulness Lessons, too. As I did, I could feel myself relaxing, and, in just a few moments, I was able to see the situation completely differently.*
>
> *My inner resistance has dissipated, and therefore the issue has, too. I had no doubt your methodology was effective, but I didn't realize how immediately transformative it could be.*
>
> *Thank you and RMT for this personal breakthrough!*

Benefits: Why Use the 7 Mindfulness Lessons?

Whether you are aware of it or not, your thoughts determine how you behave. Thoughts produce choices and behaviors, which transform you and your teammates into either collaborative allies or warring adversaries.

If you dread working with your teammates or your customers, you have placed yourself in a battleground. Battlegrounds are not necessary or useful; no one on your team really wants to be there. The 7 Mindfulness Lessons can help you rise above the battleground, transforming conflicts into solutions.

If you are among the lucky few who do not dread working with your teammates, these 7 Lessons are still relevant. They have the power to transform any circumstance or event into a fantastic learning opportunity, making every day an exciting new adventure in your classroom of life. They will undoubtedly strengthen your ability to collaborate and make better team decisions.

Your desire to improve your team situation is your motivation to apply these 7 Lessons in your work life. Use these 7 Mindfulness Lessons daily, and you rule the world you see. You maintain your power of response, frequently experience **moments of Reason**, and avoid unnecessary Ego attacks and battles. You guarantee you have no adversaries, only teammate allies.

Supportive RMT Methods

In addition to the book *7 Mindfulness Training Lessons*, the following supporting texts and tools are encouraged to ensure your team successfully applies and integrates Right-Minded Teamwork and achieves team goals.

How to Apply the Right Choice Model: Create a Right-Minded Team That Works as One

The Right Choice Model defines mindfulness as "your desire, willingness, and ability to change your attitude and behavior to effectively respond to difficult team situations." The 7 Mindfulness Lessons are woven into the recommended application for the Right Choice Model.

Right-Minded Teamwork in Any Team: The Ultimate Team-Building Method to Create a Team That Works as One

The 5 Elements, which form the core of Right-Minded Teamwork, provide excellent context for applying the 7 Lessons. Actively applying the 7 Lessons in team-building workshops will help your team create psychological goals (Element #2) and Work Agreements (Element #3).

How to Facilitate Team Work Agreements: A Practical, 10-Step Process for Building a Right-Minded Team That Works as One

Your team's Work Agreements are essentially behavioral descriptions of the 7 Mindfulness Lessons, written in your team's own words.

Right-Minded Teamwork: *9 Right Choices for Building a Team That Works as One*

This book is a valuable Right-Minded Teamwork primer. Many team leaders and facilitators ask all teammates to read this short book before the first Right-Minded Teamwork workshop. The philosophy behind the 7 Lessons, though not explicitly mentioned, is woven throughout the 9 Right Choices.

Design a Right-Minded, Team-Building Workshop: *12 Steps to Create a Team That Works as One*

For a team study approach to the 7 Mindfulness Lessons, follow these 12 steps to design your Right-Minded Teamwork workshops. Such workshops will include opportunities for teammates to briefly discuss and advocate for applying the 7 Mindfulness Lessons to challenging team situations.

Achieve Your Organization's Strategic Plan: *Create a Right-Minded Team Management System to Ensure All Teams Work as One*

Mindfulness is universal; it can benefit your entire organization. When you implement an enterprise Team Management System [TMS] that incorporates the 7 Mindfulness Lessons, teammates remain Right-Minded, allowing them to work more cohesively and productively toward team goals.

Right-Minded Teamwork: 9 Right Choices

Overview

This book is a fast read and an excellent Right-Minded Teamwork primer. It is a terrific way to introduce RMT to teammates.

These nine teamwork choices are universal, self-evident, and self-validating.

You want them in your team.

9 Right-Minded Choices

In the book ***Right-Minded Teamwork****: 9 Right Choices for Building a Team that Works as One,* each of the nine choices is defined, and exercises for applying them are provided.

Here is a brief description of each choice:

1. ***Make the Right Choice*** *(because all others rest on this one).*

To begin, all teammates discuss and enthusiastically agree to take responsibility for creating and following their custom version of Right-Minded Teamwork.

2. **Oneness or Separateness**: *Choose to behave as One.*

Your team will not live these first two choices perfectly straight away, but making a wholehearted commitment to Oneness is a crucial first step. As your team practices choosing Oneness, be patient. Be persistent. Conduct continuous improvement workshops every three months to encourage Oneness through Right-Minded Teamwork.

3. **Right-Minded communication** *ends separateness.*

In a Right-Minded team, teammates' communication is effective and kind. They do no harm. They strive to build oneness. Right-Minded communication flows naturally and effortlessly when teammates actively live the first two choices.

4. **Meaningful vision** *is essential to make your team's dream come true.*

Your team's vision provides the context for choosing Right-Minded behaviors and identifying and executing your team's continuous improvement operating system.

5. **Work Agreements** *bring teammates together as One.*

A team that actively lives its Work Agreements is a team that has established an environment in which teammates forgive past mistakes in the present. These teams have the power to achieve their full potential in the future.

6. ***Right-Minded teams adopt a "critical few" attitude*** *that ensures they complete important tasks first.*

The full-plate syndrome does not tempt or distract Right-Minded Teammates. Instead, they rise above the battleground of busyness by spending their time doing the right things right. They know that trying to do everything is not job security. It is insecurity.

7. ***Mistakes happen;*** *correct them, don't punish teammates.*

It is natural and safe for Right-Minded teammates to correct mistakes because they know that doing so is one of the most sensible and sane ways to learn. Right-Minded teammates do not fear blame; they look for solutions and focus on growth.

8. ***Conflict happens****: Embrace a classroom mindset and avoid a battleground attitude.*

When team conflict occurs, and it will, Right-Minded teammates rise above the psychological battleground, make Right-Minded choices, and find constructive solutions.

9. ***Positive recognition*** *makes it easier to keep striving to achieve the vision.*

Giving and receiving authentic recognition for a job well-done feeds team spirit and fuels the Right-Minded Teamwork continuous improvement process.

How to Apply the 9 Right Choices in Your Team

There is no one right way to apply the 9 Right Choices, but here are two possible application scenarios.

Ask all teammates to read the book ***Right-Minded Teamwork****: 9 Right Choices for Building a Team that Works as One* and complete the survey at the end. Compile teammates' scores and comments and distribute the results to all teammates. As a full team, identify the choices you want to apply to your team.

Alternately, in a team meeting, openly discuss the first two of the nine choices. By the end of the meeting, teammates will have chosen several attitudes and work behaviors to live by going forward. Capture those choices in team Work Agreements.

Throughout this short **9 Right Choices** book, within each choice, you will find a *Leader & Teammate Actions* section that offers suggested actions you can take. By the time you finish reading the last choice, **trust your intuition** as to the best way for you to apply these choices in your team. That may mean following the suggested steps in the book, or it may not. I am confident, that by the time you read and understand these choices, you, the powerful Decision-Maker that you are, will make the best choice for your team.

Regardless of your chosen approach, remember: ***It is about the dialogue***. These choices are undoubtedly important. But they are secondary to your team's dialogue about them. The goal is to produce a healthy, functional, and empowering team conversation that moves your teammates towards acting and behaving as one. The 9 Right Choices serve as catalysts for your teammate discussions and the eventual creation of team Work Agreements.

Benefits: Why Apply the 9 Right Choices?

When you apply these choices in your team, you will have consciously chosen your team's "thought system," thus defining your set of right attitudes and behaviors for achieving your team goals.

With this clarity, unified teamwork becomes effortless, and achieving team goals is inevitable.

Supportive RMT Methods

In addition to the book ***Right-Minded Teamwork****: 9 Right Choices for Building a Team that Works as One*, the following supporting texts and tools are encouraged to ensure your team successfully applies and integrates Right-Minded Teamwork and achieves team goals.

Right-Minded Teamwork in Any Team*: The Ultimate Team-Building Method to Create a Team That Works as One*

This is the core RMT framework, comprised of the 5 Elements. You may find it helpful to share this model as context for applying the 9 Right Choices. Additionally, applying the 9 Right Choices will help you successfully implement RMT's core framework and team operating system.

How to Facilitate Team Work Agreements*: A Practical, 10-Step Process for Building a Right-Minded Team That Works as One*

Your team's Work Agreements are essentially behavioral descriptions of your team's version of the 9 Right Choices.

How to Apply the Right Choice Model*: Create a Right-Minded Team That Works as One*

This teaching model shows you how to successfully apply the 9 Right Choices.

7 Mindfulness Training Lessons*: Improve Teammates' Ability to Work as One with Right-Minded Thinking*

Learning and applying these 7 Mindfulness Lessons helps your team effectively apply the 9 Right Choices.

Design a Right-Minded, Team-Building Workshop: *12 Steps to Create a Team That Works as One*

Follow these 12 steps to design a 9 Right Choices workshop.

Achieve Your Organization's Strategic Plan: *Create a Right-Minded Team Management System to Ensure All Teams Work as One*

When you implement an enterprise Team Management System [TMS] built on the 9 Right Choices, teammates regularly focus on Right-Minded solutions, improving team productivity and achieving team goals.

Design a Right-Minded, Team-Building Workshop

Overview

This book will teach you how to design a practical, real-world, Right-Minded, team-building workshop.

Right-Minded Teamwork does not advocate team games, outdoor exercises, or social events as legitimate substitutes for team building. They can be fun, but they are indirect and do not resolve a team's real issues.

Right-Minded Team building is not a game-based or social approach to team building. It is a "real-world" method that actually works.

Though this book is written primarily for team facilitators, leaders, and teammates can also easily follow the steps to design a successful team workshop.

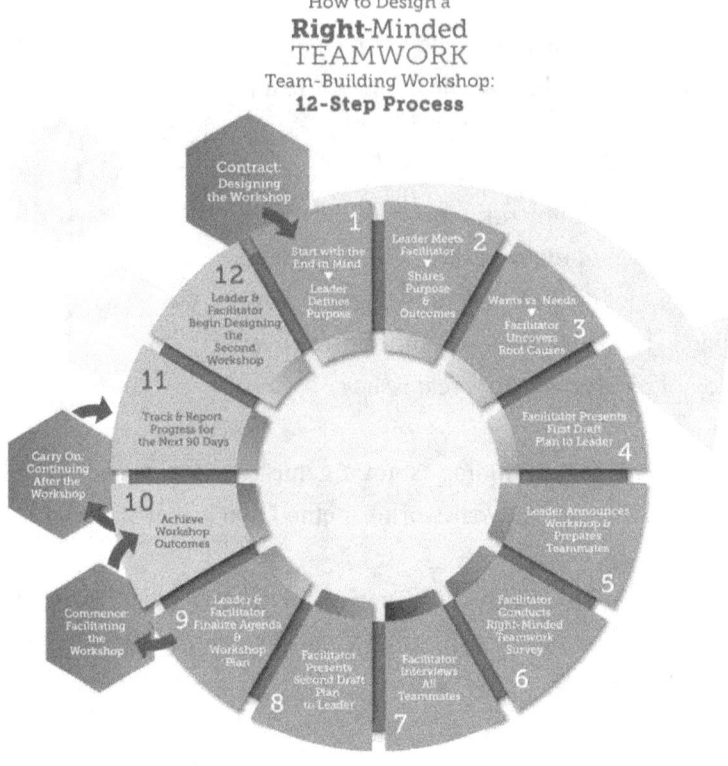

Overview: 12 Steps, Three Phases

The RMT process includes 12 steps presented in three phases:

Contract: Designing the workshop (steps 1-9)
Commence: Facilitating the workshop (step 10)
Carry On: Keeping up momentum after the workshop (steps 11-12)

For full details on all 12 Steps, consult the book. For now, here is a high-level description.

Contract: Designing the Workshop (steps 1-9)

Step 1

To begin, the team leader determines the workshop's purpose. Usually, workshops focus on something the team needs to change or improve because teammates are not working together as one.

Step 2

The leader conveys the purpose and potential outcomes of the workshop to the facilitator. Both agree to follow the 12-step process to design the workshop.

Step 3

The leader gives the facilitator permission to think of their initial desired outcomes as symptoms, allowing the facilitator to uncover root causes the leader may not have considered. It's not unusual between steps 3 & 7 to learn that what the leader said they initially wanted may not be what the team needs.

Step 4

The facilitator creates and presents a 1st Draft Plan to the leader. The plan includes the initial set of workshop outcomes, agenda, Punch List of workshop topics, and a workshop announcement plan.

Step 5

The leader announces the workshop and prepares teammates. Teammates learn the facilitator will interview them. By offering their input and perspective, teammates will eagerly participate in designing the workshop outcomes and agenda.

Step 6

The facilitator conducts a Right-Minded Teammate survey to help identify potential workshop outcomes.

Step 7

The facilitator interviews all teammates, summarizing their collective views in the Punch List document.

Step 8

The facilitator creates and presents a 2nd Draft Plan to the leader.

Step 9

The leader and facilitator fine-tune and agree on the final outcomes and workshop agenda. Together, they distribute the agenda and begin preparing teammates for the workshop.

Commence: Facilitating the Workshop (step 10)

Step 10

The leader and facilitator conduct the workshop and achieve workshop outcomes.

Teammates agree to track their performance after the workshop. They agree on what they will track, how they will track it, and to whom they will report their progress. They agree to conduct team-building workshops every 90 days.

Carry On: Keeping Up Momentum (steps 11-12)

Step 11

For the next 90 days, the team implements their tasks and tracks their progress.

Step 12

The leader and facilitator either begin designing the second workshop or transfer that responsibility to others.

The cycle continues onward, beginning with Step 1 again.

As this cycle is repeated over time, the team grows and evolves into a team that consistently works as one.

Benefits: Why Use the 12 Steps Process?

Because this workshop-building method engages teammates in the design and agenda, it virtually guarantees teammates cannot wait to attend their team-building workshop. They know their time will be productive, and beneficial and will allow them to get real work done.

If you are a team leader, your teammates will appreciate the straightforward process that includes them in the workshop design. Their confidence and trust in your leadership will increase.

If you are a team-building facilitator, your clients will love this method because they quickly see its value. Additionally, they will know you are helping them build a Right-Minded team that achieves its goals and produces results.

Supportive RMT Methods

In addition to the book *Design a Right-Minded, Team-Building Workshop: 12 Steps to Create a Team That Works as One*, the following supporting texts and tools are encouraged to ensure your team successfully applies and integrates Right-Minded Teamwork and achieves team goals.

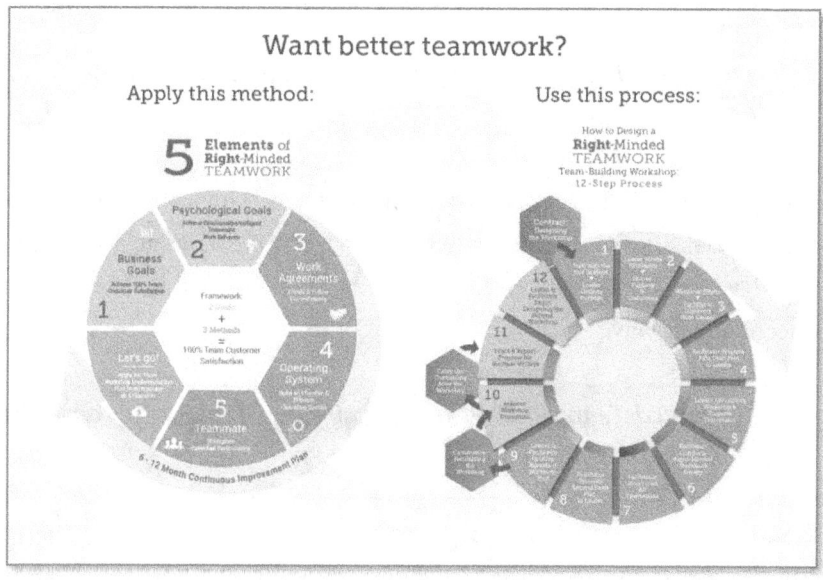

Right-Minded Teamwork in Any Team: *The Ultimate Team-Building Method to Create a Team That Works as One*

This is the core RMT framework, comprised of the 5 Elements. You may find it helpful to share this model as context for what the team will accomplish through the workshop they are developing using the 12 Steps.

How to Facilitate Team Work Agreements: *A Practical, 10-Step Process for Building a Right-Minded Team That Works as One*

Work Agreements are a probable outcome of a Right-Minded Teamwork team-building workshop. To help lay the groundwork for this result, the leader and facilitator can start to communicate the value of creating Work Agreements during the planning and design process for the upcoming workshop.

How to Apply the Right Choice Model: *Create a Right-Minded Team That Works as One*

As you discuss the workshop with the team, you can briefly show teammates the Right Choice Model and emphasize that a key team goal is for all teammates to act and behave in a Right-Minded and accountable way.

Right-Minded Teamwork: *9 Right Choices for Building a Team That Works as One*

You can opt to give teammates a copy of this book as a pre-read for the workshop, or briefly show teammates the 9 Right Choices during workshop preparation.

7 Mindfulness Training Lessons: *Improve Teammates' Ability to Work as One with Right-Minded Thinking*

As you are interviewing teammates, you may show teammates these 7 Lessons, sharing that when they are applied, they will help the team work together as one.

Achieve Your Organization's Strategic Plan*: Create a Right-Minded Team Management System to Ensure All Teams Work as One*

When you implement an enterprise Team Management System [TMS], ask your leaders and team facilitators to use the 12 Steps as they share Right-Minded Teamwork with their teams through team-building workshops. Doing so will most certainly increase the likelihood of creating a wildly successful Team Management System and cohesive enterprise that works as one.

Achieve Your Organization's Strategic Plan

Overview

An enterprise's Team Management System (TMS) aligns the entire organization's attitudes and work behavior. An effective TMS ensures everyone is doing their part to achieve the company's vision, mission, and strategic goals.

There are four phases to creating and deploying your organization's customized TMS, each described in this book. Your TMS will support Right-Minded Teamwork in every team in your enterprise.

Phase 1 – Executive Leadership launches TMS

Phase 2 – Steering Team creates, organizes, and pilots the TMS

Phase 3 – Measure performance and roll TMS out to all teams

Phase 4 – Continue TMS for growth & sustainability

How RMT's Team Management System Works

TMS is much like your employee performance management system but on a team level. Every team in the enterprise sets performance goals that align with and help achieve the enterprise's strategic plan.

Every quarter, each team measures and reports its actual progress toward achieving those goals.

The following teams should be initially involved in establishing the organization's TMS:
- Executive Leadership
- TMS Steering Team
- Internal team-building facilitators

Eventually, the TMS is rolled out across the organization, and all teams participate.

How to Apply a Team Management System

The four phases of a sustainable RMT Team Management System.

Phase 1 – Executive Leadership launches TMS

- RMT is implemented in the executive team.
- RMT is adopted as the enterprise's standard teamwork process.
- Executives establish a Steering Team that will start up and initially manage the TMS.

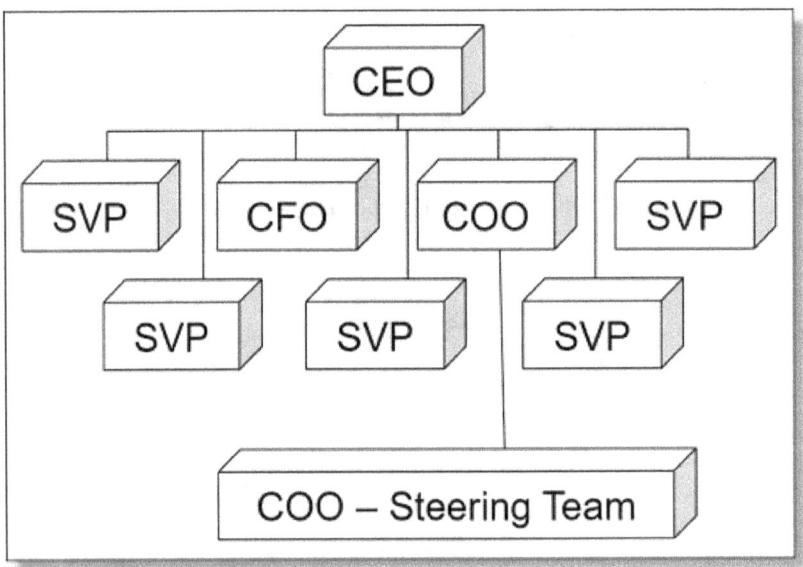

Phase 2 – Steering Team creates, organizes, and pilots the TMS

- The Steering Team creates the enterprise's startup TMS.
- Select individual teammates to become TMS team-building facilitators.
- They pilot the startup TMS in a few teams.
- The Steering Team fine-tunes the TMS in preparation for a broader enterprise rollout.
- Over time, TMS is rolled out throughout the organization until all teams are participating.
- Using the Right-Minded Teamwork method, the Steering Team continues to manage the TMS towards Phase 4.

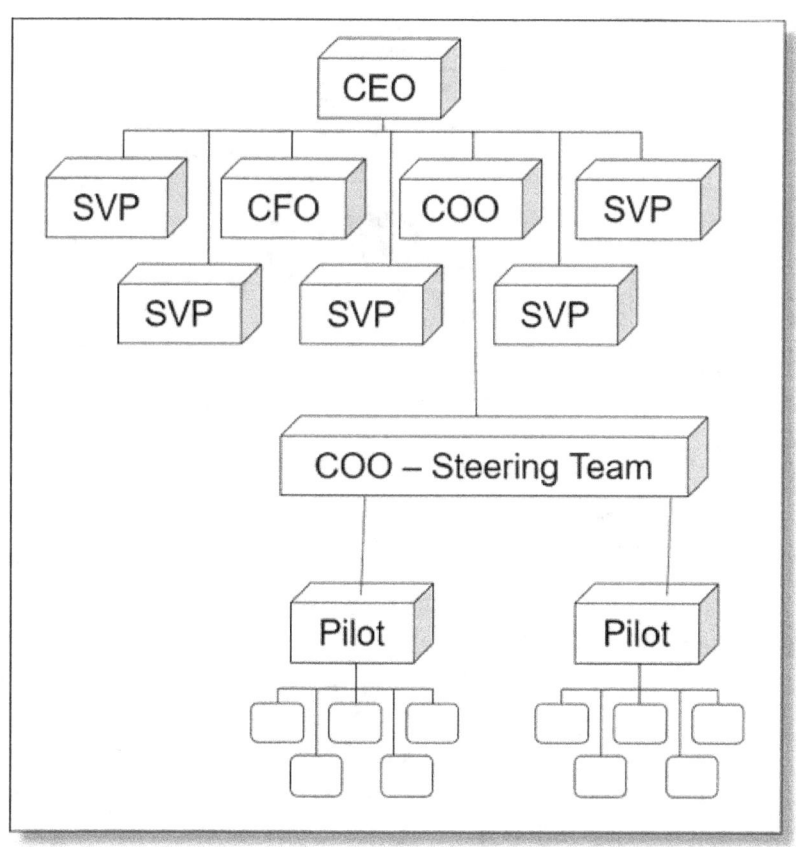

Phase 3 – Measure performance and roll out the TMS to all teams

- Within three to four months after startup, the first quarterly TMS results are reported.
- The TMS is rolled out to more teams within the first 12 to 18 months.
- Within 24 months, TMS quarterly reports demonstrate beneficial enterprise results.
- Results are communicated internally and externally.

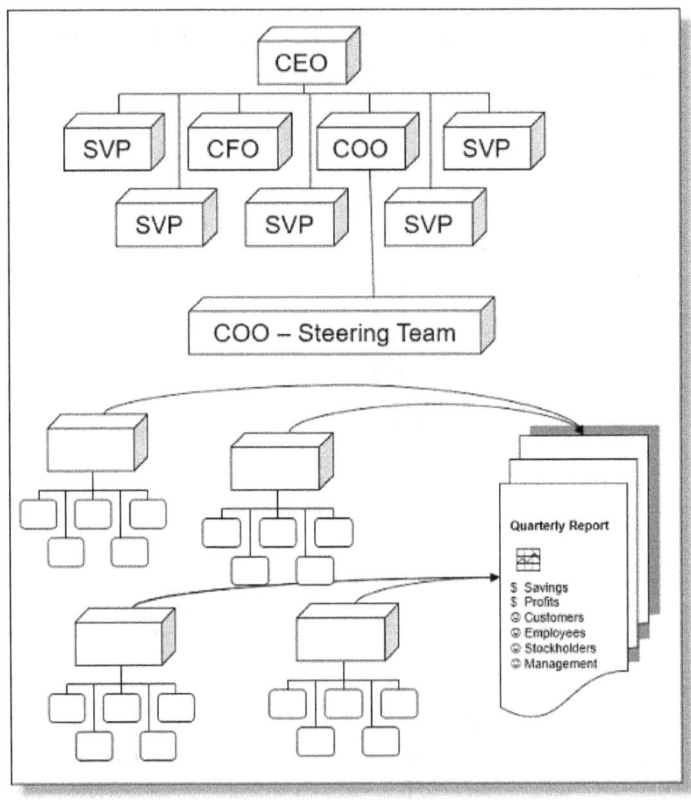

Phase 4 – Continue TMS for growth and sustainability

- The Steering Team is transformed into a stable growth and management phase with the executive team's support and guidance.
- Some original members are transferred to new opportunities, while other new members are chosen to lead and manage the TMS department.
- New reporting and governance structures are established.
- The new TMS leadership team uses RMT's continuous improvement Team Operating System to manage the TMS going forward.

Benefits: Why Establish an RMT-Based Team Management System?

When an enterprise has a strong Team Management System, you increase the likelihood that every team is aligned with the enterprise's strategic plan, thus operating with focused clarity. This enterprise-wide alignment ensures all teams are pulling the organization in the same direction. Consequently, the organization regularly achieves a higher percentage of its strategic goals year over year.

Within the first six to 12 months, RMT's version of a TMS will begin paying for itself. Within the first 18 to 24 months, TMS will report consistent and demonstrable enterprise-wide results.

These results, when communicated internally, will foster employee motivation and pride.

When communicated externally, the enterprise's reputation and stature increase.

Supportive RMT Methods

In addition to the book *Achieve Your Organization's Strategic Plan: Create a Right-Minded Team Management System to Ensure All Teams Work as One*, the following supporting texts and tools are encouraged to ensure your team successfully applies and integrates Right-Minded Teamwork and achieves team goals.

***Right-Minded Teamwork in Any Team**: The Ultimate Team-Building Method to Create a Team That Works as One*

This is the core RMT framework, comprised of the 5 Elements. Right-Minded Teamwork and the 5 Elements are essential to the day-to-day functionality of the TMS program.

***How to Facilitate Team Work Agreements:** A Practical, 10-Step Process for Building a Right-Minded Team That Works as One*

This book will significantly help your organization in planning and designing your TMS. Through team-building workshops focused on Work Agreements, your teams will create their own Right-Minded rules and moral codes to live and work by. During these workshops, the Steering Team will also train internal team facilitators who can take over and continue facilitating Work Agreement workshops going forward.

Design a Right-Minded, Team-Building Workshop: *12 Steps to Create a Team That Works as One*

In this book, team facilitators will learn and follow the 12 essential steps to design workshops teammates actually want to attend. When team leaders and facilitators partner and apply these steps, they create a Right-Minded environment conducive to addressing real problems and achieving real-world goals.

How to Apply the Right Choice Model*: Create a Right-Minded Team That Works as One*

This model will teach leaders, teammates, and facilitators how to act and behave in a Right-Minded way while using the TMS. When this model is applied, collaboration, accountability, and productive teamwork are the natural result.

Right-Minded Teamwork*: 9 Right Choices for Building a Team That Works as One*

This short and easy-to-read book is an excellent RMT primer. The organization and Steering Team may consider giving a copy to all teammates as a pre-read for their first RMT workshop.

7 Mindfulness Training Lessons: *Improve Teammates' Ability to Work as One with Right-Minded Thinking*

These 7 Mindfulness Lessons encourage leaders and teammates to own their behaviors, take control of their minds, and learn to consistently act in a Right-Minded and accountable way.

The End.
Your New Beginning.

When all 5 Elements of Right-Minded Teamwork's core framework are fully released into your team's operating system, you have established the proper condition for your new beginning towards successfully achieving Right-Minded Teamwork.

You are now thinking and behaving in a Right-Minded way. You are self-aware and focused on achieving your team's business and psychological goals. You consistently strive for 100% customer satisfaction, and you always aim to **do no harm** while **working as one**.

To guide your steps, you have purposeful team **Work Agreements** describing your team's thought system. You get work done by leveraging your **Team Operating System**, identifying the critical-few, focusing on solutions, and making true improvements.

As Right-Minded Teammates, you **willfully follow Reason**, behave mindfully, and positively navigate difficult team situations. You have risen above Ego's battleground to joyfully engage with each other in your work classroom, learning and growing every day. Happily, they find themselves living more and more often in the **Unified Circle of Right-Minded Teamwork Thinking.**

Now that you understand each of RMT's 5 Elements and how they will benefit your team, you are ready to begin implementing RMT in your team. Remember, even though there is no one right way to implement RMT, the three-workshop Implementation Plan presented earlier in these pages will always work.

So, gather your teammates, and conduct your first workshop. Live your new team Work Agreements for a month or two, and then conduct the second workshop. Trust in the process, and keep moving forward.

When you finish the third teammate development workshop, your team will begin following your customized 90-Day team operating plan. Every quarter, you will get to measure your progress and success. Each time, you will reinforce the value of RMT in your team.

Don't Forget!

As you begin your journey to Right-Minded Teamwork, don't forget:

Good teamwork does not just happen on its own. It must be cultivated, tended, and encouraged.

To bring your team together, you need guidance from proven, real-world methods, such as Right-Minded Teamwork. Moreover, you and your teammates must sincerely want to receive and follow this guidance, or the powerful teachings will be meaningless. Good teamwork is a collaborative venture of commitment and growth. You know this to be true.

If you want better teamwork, Right-Minded Teamwork can show you how to get there and what to do, but only with your help. Together with your teammates, you must believe that you have what it takes. With that conviction and Reason's guidance, you will collectively create and sustain Right-Minded Teamwork.

Now, go and create Right-Minded Teamwork for yourself and your team, and know that *you are making the world better for everyone, everywhere, forever.*

The End

Thanks for reading our Right-Minded Teamwork book. If you enjoyed it, wouldn't you please take a moment to leave a review at your favorite retailer or RightMindedTeamwork.com?

Now here is something especially useful: a *Glossary of Right-Minded Teamwork Terms and Resources.*

And finally, on behalf of Reason and all the Right-Minded Teammate Decision-Makers, we extend our best wishes to you and your teammates as you create another *Right-Minded Team that Works Together as One.*

Glossary of Right-Minded Teamwork Terms & Resources

This is an abbreviated list. The longer list is in all our other books.

A Course in Miracles

Oneness. Forgiveness is the key to happiness, inner peace, undifferentiated unity, and ultimately – *oneness*. "A Course In Miracles (ACIM) is a unique spiritual self-study program designed to awaken us to the truth of our *oneness* with God and Love," as posted on ACIM.org and ACIM.org/ACIM/en. See the Foundation for A Course in Miracles at FACIM.org, where Ken Wapnick, the founder, created this beautiful definition.

> *"A Course in Miracles is a psychological approach to spirituality where forgiveness is the central theme, and inner peace is the result."*

ACIM and other moral and spiritual philosophies that advocate and help people everywhere **work together as One** has inspired Right-Minded Teamwork.

We used Ken's definition as a guide to creating the Right-Minded Teamwork definition.

> *Right-Minded Teamwork is a business-oriented, psychological approach to team building where acceptance, forgiveness, and adjustments are teammate characteristics and 100% customer satisfaction is the team's result.*

All Right-Minded Teamwork methods, processes, and tools seamlessly work together to help you create and sustain a *Team That Works Together as* **One**.

Accept, Forgive, Adjust

These three terms are at the core of Right-Minded Teammate attitudes and behaviors. These verbs are also central to the 7 Mindfulness Training Lessons, which are summed up in the sentence, 'Right-Minded Teammates **accept**, **forgive**, and **adjust** their thinking and work behavior."

Furthermore, these three concepts are included in the definition of Right-Minded Teamwork:

> *Right-Minded Teamwork is a business-oriented, psychological approach to team building where acceptance, forgiveness, and adjustment are teammate characteristics, and 100% customer satisfaction is the team's result.*

Lastly, these terms are also incorporated as three of the five steps in the Right Choice Model, which describes accountable and responsible Right-Minded Teamwork behavior.

Ally or Adversary Teammate

Right-Minded Teamwork asserts that as teammates, you either work together as allies or pull apart, viewing each other as adversaries.

Allies work towards achieving team goals. Adversaries work towards individual elevation, which separates and divides the team.

To determine whether you are in an ally or adversary mindset, ask yourself, *"Do I want to be right, or do I want our team to be successful?"* Allies want to be part of a successful team. Adversaries want to be right, no matter the cost.

As an adversary, Ego persuades you to compete with your teammates. As an ally, Reason says the opposite. Reason gently reminds you that separateness prevents true success. There cannot be oneness or collaboration when there is competition.

As the Decision-Maker, you choose to follow either Reason or Ego. You either collaborate or compete. You are an ally or adversary. There is no middle ground.

If you choose to follow Reason and become an ally, you embrace and live your team's Work Agreements. If you decide to follow Ego, you become an adversary, creating a battleground inside yourself and your team.

To transform competitive adversaries into collaborative allies, start by following the Right Choice Model, creating team Work Agreements, and applying the 7 Mindfulness Training Lessons.

Avoidance Behavior

Even though the term "avoidance behavior" is not often mentioned in the Right-Minded Teamwork model or books, avoidance behavior is easy to detect in teammates. If you notice it occurring, from an RMT perspective, you can consider it wrong-minded, adversarial behavior.

Identifying avoidance behaviors and attitudes and understanding the harm they cause is the first step in moving from a wrong-minded place into Right-Mindedness. The 7 Mindfulness Training Lessons and the Right Choice Model are excellent tools for teaching yourself and your team how to act and behave in a Right-Minded, accountable way.

For example, if you look carefully at the Right Choice Model's lower loop, you will notice that when a difficult situation occurs, the victim or victimizer first avoids the situation.

When Right-Minded Teammates ask themselves the Right Choice Model question, "How did I **create**, **promote**, or **allow** this difficult situation to happen?" they often realize they have unconsciously demonstrated avoidance behavior. Then, noticing their mistake, they simply choose to **accept**, **forgive**, and **adjust** their approach and return to living in accordance with their team Work Agreements.

Battleground:
Where People Are Punished for Mistakes

The battleground represents wrong-minded thinking. It is a mental attitude or thought system that defends and encourages adversarial behaviors such as blame and attack.

Think of the battleground as a psychological symbol for those moments when you realize you are listening to Ego, not Reason (like when you notice avoidance behavior). You recognize that for whatever reason, you are having an Ego attack and have made the wrong-minded choice. When you are in the battleground, you "punish" others for their mistakes, either by victimizing others or becoming a victim yourself.

When you are in your right mind, on the other hand, you see your team as a lovely and safe classroom, the opposite of the battleground. You do not punish others. You choose, instead, to rise above the conflict.

The purpose of recognizing the battlegrounds in your mind is to own the pain that you are causing yourself which helps you recognize that you consciously want to leave it, overlook it, rise above it, and to transport your mind into the classroom where you return to the Unified Circle of Right-Minded Thinking with your teammates.

Right-Minded Teammates working in safe and supportive classrooms do not fight, blame, or punish. Instead, they choose oneness over separateness. They are committed to the team's success and achieving team goals.

To overcome a battleground in yourself or your team, go to RightMindedTeamwork.com, or visit your favorite book retailer to pick up your copy of **How to Apply the Right Choice Model**: *Create a Right-Minded Team That Works as One*. Inside, you will find a list of battleground attitudes and behaviors as well as the costs and benefits of classroom versus battleground thinking and behaving.

Certified Master Facilitator (CMF)

The Certified Master Facilitator (CMF) credential is a mark of excellence for facilitators. It is the highest available certification for facilitators.

To learn more or to find a certified facilitator worldwide, visit the International Institute for Facilitation at INIFAC.org.

Classroom:
Where People Learn from Mistakes

Like the battleground, the classroom is a symbol. But unlike the battlefield, where people punish or are punished, the classroom is where you learn and find inspiration.

At some point in your past, you have experienced the joy and wonder of learning. Right-Minded Teamwork invites you to view your team as a safe place to experience this wonder and joy as you learn new teamwork skills and collaborate to achieve team goals.

When you are experiencing fear in any form, or you realize you are having an Ego attack, you are in the battleground. To enter the classroom instead, say to yourself,

There is nothing to fear. In my mind, I choose to rise above this silly battleground and head to my Right-Minded classroom. There, we are committed to do no harm, and work as one. There, I will find solutions.

REASON, EGO & THE RIGHT-MINDED TEAMWORK MYTH · 149

By recognizing the fear behind your Ego attack and reminding yourself to return to the classroom, you experience a **moment of Reason**. You also strengthen your Right-Minded thought system and restore yourself to Right-Minded Thinking.

In the RMT book *How to Apply the Right Choice Model: Create a Right-Minded Team That Works as One,* you will find a list of 30 Right-Minded and wrong-minded attitudes and behaviors, plus the associated costs and benefits to your team.

Communication Work Agreement

What you think – *your thought system* – drives your communication in one of two ways. You either communicate as a collaborative ally or as a competitive, dysfunctional, and emotionally immature adversary.

Teams that work as one and achieve their goals regularly seek out opportunities to improve communication. They take positive action by creating and living a Communication Work Agreement that describes their team's agreed-upon communication style.

Right-Minded communication is a core concept in the book ***Right-Minded Teamwork**: 9 Right Choices for Building a Team That Works as One,* available at RightMindedTeamwork.com or your favorite book retailer. To create your team's Communication Work Agreement, follow the suggestions in the book ***How to Facilitate Teamwork Agreements**: A Practical, 10-Step Process for Building a Right-Minded Team That Works as One.* In there, you will find two real examples of which one is a team Communication Work Agreement.

Create, Promote, Allow

These three concepts form the foundation of the Right Choice Model's essential question:

> How have I **created**, **promoted**, or **allowed** this situation to occur?

Asking and honestly answering this question ensures teammates are "owning their part" in a difficult situation.

High-performing Right-Minded Teammates always ask themselves this question because it leads them to solutions. It is a clear demonstration of the RMT motto, "Do No Harm. Work as One.®"

Critical Few:
Complete Important Tasks First

When a team is stuck in "full plate syndrome," identifying and completing the critical few - those tasks that have the largest and most direct impact on the team's success - is key to moving forward.

At the root of full plate syndrome is the **team's collective fear**, driven by Ego, that declares you will get in trouble if you do not do it all... even though the truth is you can never do it all.

People who listen to Ego believe they do not have a choice. Rather than realistically prioritizing their workload, they punish themselves for failing to meet the unreasonable goal of completing everything. They drain their energy, lose their focus, and make mistakes. They become powerless, cynical, and burned out.

But Reason reminds us that we always have this choice:

> *We can either win by doing the critical few tasks, or we can lose by attempting to do everything.*

Spend more time doing the right things right, and let go of low-value tasks. Holding on to lower-value tasks is **not security**. It is **incarceration**.

The concept of the "critical few" is introduced in greater depth in the book ***Right-Minded Teamwork****: 9 Right Choices for Building a Team That Works as One*.

See **Recognition: Make It Easy to Keep Going** for a related concept.

Decision-Maker: The Real You

Ken Wapnick, Ph.D., created the term "Decision-Maker" to define the "real you" in *A Course in Miracles*. For more on his work, visit FACIM.org.

Within Right-Minded Teamwork, the Right Choice Model uses the term "Decision-Maker" to describe the part of you that chooses to listen to and follow either the wrong-minded ways of Ego or the Right-Minded ways of Reason.

> *Your Decision-Maker is 100% responsible for who you choose to follow, what you choose to think, and how you choose to behave.*

Right-Mindedness is achieved when you listen to and follow Reason. Listening means calming your Ego mind, trusting your intuition, and allowing space for a **moment of Reason** to arise.

When Right-Mindedness becomes an integral part of a team, the team consistently works together as one, doing no harm, within the forgiving Unified Circle of Right-Minded Thinking. This is Right-Minded Teamwork.

Decision-Maker: Trust Your Intuition

If thinking about Reason and Ego is new to you, it can be helpful to think of Reason as your positive intuition and Ego as your negative, arrogant, and sometimes vindictive intuition.

At different times throughout our lives, we all listen to and follow each of these teachers.

Stop and remember when you had a hunch or a feeling as to what you should do or say in a particular situation. Did you ignore your intuition? Let's say you did not follow your instinct, and it turned out to be a mistake. What did you say to yourself and others?

>   *I wish I had trusted my intuition!*

As this memory illustrates, **you already know how to listen and be mindful** of your intuition. It is your natural, pre-separation state of mind [See **Oneness vs. Separateness**].

You just need to do it regularly.

Decision-Making Work Agreement

Every team needs a Decision-Making Work Agreement that clearly defines how decisions are made and who makes them. It makes good business sense to create a general agreement and put it into your team's Operating System as a team Work Agreement.

If you do not currently have a Decision-Making agreement or you have not updated your agreement, I highly recommend you do that as soon as it is practical.

In the book, ***How to Facilitate Team Work Agreements****: A Practical, 10-Step Process for Building a Right-Minded Team That Works as One,* you will find two real agreement examples. The first one is a behavioral team Communication Work Agreement, and the other is a Decision-Making Work Agreement. Check it out and use it as a model for your team's Decision-Making Work Agreement.

Desire & Willingness: Preconditions for Accountability

Even though the terms "desire" and "willingness" are not often mentioned in Right-Minded Teamwork materials (except within the Right Choice Model), Right-Mindedness and accountability are virtually synonymous.

The concepts of desire and willingness permeate all RMT methods and processes simply because it is impossible to think in a Right-Minded way, behave with Right-Minded Accountability, and achieve Right-Minded Teamwork without a heartfelt desire and genuine willingness to do so.

The Right Choice Model and the book ***How to Apply the Right Choice Model****: Create a Right-Minded Team That Works as One* both teach, "Right-Minded Accountability is the desire and willingness to change my mind and behavior in order to effectively respond to difficult team situations."

If you share the Right Choice Model with your team and distribute the Right Choice cards to teammates, you will see the definition of "desire and willingness" on the cards.

Do No Harm. Work as One. ®

The Right-Minded philosophy is founded on two universal truths:

None of us is as smart as all of us.
Right-Minded Teammates know that working collaboratively together, in a Right-Minded manner, is the only way to create the kind of teamwork that achieves and sustains 100% customer satisfaction.

Do no harm and work as one.
As a Right-Minded Teammate, you can be firm, direct, gentle, and compassionate, all at the same time. You do not blame yourself or others for mistakes. You and your teammates are allies, not adversaries, working together towards your shared goals.

Ego & Ego Attack

Ego is the negative, wrong-minded teacher who continually tells you how difficult the world is and how you must constantly fight to survive. Reason is the opposite of Ego. Reason teaches you to "do unto others as you would have them do unto you."

Ego believes everyone is out to get you and directs you to "do unto others *before* they do unto you." Ego is also the creator of the tiny, mad idea of separation presented in the Right-Minded Teamwork Myth.

An Ego attack is a flash of negative, out-of-control emotion. It happens when you believe the awful feeling you are experiencing has been caused by something someone else said or did to you. Without thinking, you become behaviorally triggered; your body language, tone of voice, and the words you say become mean-spirited. An Ego attack is the opposite of a **moment of Reason**.

As soon as you realize you are experiencing an Ego attack, you must train your mind to say, *"I am angry. I have lost control. I am out of my right mind. I need a moment of Reason to gain control of my attitude. I must return to the classroom so I can find a Right-Minded way of replying that allows us to do no harm and work as one."*

Moment of Reason

When you are facing a challenge such as an Ego attack, and you experience a positive and perhaps surprising moment of revelation, clarity, or sanity, you have achieved a moment of Reason.

These moments occur when you genuinely try to move from the battleground into the classroom. When Reason's teaching breaks through, you move from wrong-mindedness into Right-Mindedness.

Moments of Reason are magnificent. They are a cornerstone of your Right-Minded thought system. When they happen, you feel confident and at peace. You know what you should do, what to say, and to whom.

In moments of Reason, you know beyond a shadow of a doubt that you want and need your teammates. You are easily able to return to the Unified Circle of Right-Minded Thinking, where teammates forgive one another, do no harm, and work as one.

Onboarding New Teammates

When a new person, leader, or teammate, joins your team, it is vitally important to properly onboard them within their first week on the job. In a single short meeting where everyone attends, the onboarding is easily and effectively accomplished. Present all your RMT goals and Work Agreements along with why they were created. They ask you clarifying questions. Afterward, you ask them to accept the team's goals and actively live the team's Work Agreements.

Oneness vs. Separateness

Oneness is a psychological state of mind. It can be described in many ways using phrases such as, "None of us is as smart as all of us," or, "do no harm, and work as one."

Separateness is the opposite of oneness. To become a Right-Minded teammate, you must train your mind to choose attitudes and behaviors that create and extend oneness, not separateness. For a list of 30 examples of oneness, see the Right-Minded Teamwork Attitudes & Behaviors list found in numerous RMT books.

The concepts and story behind oneness and separateness are introduced in RMT's book, **Reason, Ego & the Right-Minded Teamwork Myth:** *The Philosophy and Process for Creating a Right-Minded Team That Works Together as One.*

In this book, you will learn about Ego's "tiny, mad idea" of wanting more "stuff" and how Ego's choices led us all into a world of separation. That tiny, mad moment was, literally, the **birth of separation**. But, as the Myth reveals, Reason is always ready to lead us back into oneness - our pre-separation state – joyfully described as the Unified Circle of Right-Minded Thinking where we can do no harm and work as one.

Psychological Goals

A team's psychological goals describe how teammates intentionally choose to think and behave as they work together to achieve their team's business goals.

Psychological goals, such as achieving mutual trust and respect among teammates, may be viewed as a team's collective school of thought, values, or thought system.

These consciously chosen goals, captured in team Work Agreements, clarify the principles or standards of behavior for the team.

Here is a specific example of a psychological goal you will find in a number of RMT materials:

> *When difficult team situations happen, we accept, forgive, and adjust our attitudes and behavior. We always find solutions because we believe that none of us is as smart as all of us.*

Reason

Reason is a mythological character and symbolic guide who shows you how to think and behave in a Right-Minded way. As your Right-Minded teacher, Reason helps you differentiate and choose between Right-Minded and wrong-minded attitudes and behaviors.

Reason is the opposite of Ego. Whereas Ego believes everyone is out to get you and instructs you to "do unto others *before* they do unto you," Reason teaches you to "do unto others as you would have them do unto you."
Ego encourages and projects separateness.
Reason cultivates and extends oneness.

Reason is that part of your mind that always speaks for the Right Choice attitudes and behaviors. When you need a **moment of Reason**, to find the best way to respond to a difficult team situation, say to yourself:

> *I am here only to be truly helpful.*
>
> *I am here to represent Reason who sent me.*
>
> *I do not have to worry about what to say or what to do because Reason who sent me will direct me.*

When you experience a moment of Reason (a moment of revelation, clarity, or sanity regarding a particular challenge), "remembering" Reason's gentle guidance towards oneness restores your mind to the forgiving Unified Circle of Right-Minded Thinking.

Recognition:
Make It Easy to Keep Going

Authentic recognition is not about bestowing company shirts and prizes. It is about giving and receiving genuine appreciation for a job well done.

Recognition plays a critical role in growing your team's business because it keeps your team's spirit ignited. Unfortunately, many people work in team environments where there is little to no recognition. These teammates are discouraged. They do not give their best to the team. Why should they?

Discouraged teammates are like racehorses. If a horse is giving you only 80%, you can whip him, and he will give you 90%. Whip him again, and he will give you 100%. But if you whip him again, after he has already given you everything he has, he will drop back to 80%, or maybe even less. He has learned that you are going to whip him regardless, even if he works harder. So why should he give you his best?

Whipped people leave teams. Far too often, the ones who leave are the most talented teammates. People who receive legitimate and genuine recognition stay and contribute. Shirts and prizes cannot earn that kind of loyalty or effort.

Recognition is a concept you will find in the book ***Right-Minded Teamwork****: 9 Right Choices for Building a Team That Works as One*. To learn more, go to RightMindedTeamwork.com.

See **Critical Few: Complete Important Tasks First**. for a related concept.

Right Choice Model

The Right Choice Model is an effective teaching aid that will help you and your teammates choose your own set of unique, "right" teamwork attitudes and behaviors.

Inspired by *A Course in Miracles*, The Right Choice Model consists of two circles. The upper loop of acceptance, forgiveness, and adjustment represents the Unified Circle of Right-Minded Thinking. The lower loop of rejection, Ego attack, and defensiveness describes the separated or divided circle of wrong-minded thinking.

To learn more about this simple but powerful teaching model, go to RightMindedTeamwork.com or your favorite book retailer, and pick up your copy of **How to Apply the Right Choice Model**: *Create a Right-Minded Team That Works as One.*

In addition to learning how to integrate the Right Choice Model on your team, you will also discover a list of 30 Right-Minded and wrong-minded attitudes and behaviors and their associated costs and benefits.

Right-Minded Teamwork ® Attitudes & Behaviors

The Right-Minded Teamwork model includes a list of 30 behavioral and process-oriented teammate attitudes and behaviors with their associated costs and benefits. I collected and compiled these over three decades of team-building workshops.

This valuable list includes clear, specific, right, and wrong behaviors "taught" to us by either Reason or Ego.

You can find the list in several RMT books, including ***How to Apply the Right Choice Model***: *Create a Right-Minded Team That Works as One*, available at RightMindedTeamwork.com or your favorite book retailer.

Right-Mindedness vs. Wrong-Mindedness

"Mindedness" is what you choose to think and perceive. Right-Mindedness refers to the positive mental state, perceptions, choices, and actions you demonstrate when following Reason's guidance. Wrong-mindedness refers to the negative mental state that occurs when you follow Ego's advice.

> *Mindfulness is a journey without distance to a goal you want to achieve.*

In the book ***How to Apply the Right Choice Model***: *Create a Right-Minded Team That Works as One*, you will find a list of rewards and consequences for choosing Right-Mindedness.

In the book ***7 Mindfulness Training Lessons**: Improve Teammates' Ability to Work as One with Right-Minded Thinking*, you will learn that in every circumstance, and especially during difficult team situations, Right-Minded Teammates practice mindfulness, or Right-Mindedness, to move them into an ally-focused way of thinking and behaving.

To bring your team back into the forgiving Unified Circle of Right-Minded Thinking, pick up your copy of either or both books at RightMindedTeamwork.com or your favorite book retailer.

Thought System

<u>What you believe *is* your thought system.</u>

Pause and reflect on this truth, and above all, be thankful that it is true.

Whether you are consciously aware of it or not, your thought system is the lens through which you view the world. Without exception, everyone has one. And though there are many variations, there are only two thought systems from which to choose:
- A Right-Minded thought system, which extends ally beliefs of acceptance, forgiveness, and adjustment to everyone, everywhere, forever
- A wrong-minded system, which projects adversarial assaults of rejection, attack, and defensiveness to everyone, everywhere, forever

Once you have developed a thought system of any kind, you live it and teach it. Even if you are not completely aware of it, it remains at the forefront of your mind, influencing your behaviors and choices every day.

If your thought system is negative, or you choose to follow Ego into unnecessary and adversarial competition, you cannot be a happy, successful teammate.

To live in the land of oneness where your workplace is a safe and supportive classroom and where you and your teammates work as one to achieve team goals, you must train your mind and align your thought system with the teachings of Reason.

There is no possible compromise between these two thought systems. You either collaborate, or you compete. When you follow Ego, you take your team to the battleground. When you choose to follow Reason, you willingly create and genuinely strive to live your team's Work Agreements. With Reason's help, you transform your team into a lovely, collaborative, successful classroom.

The choice is clear. Reject Ego. Embrace Reason. Be Thankful.

Train Your Mind

When your mind is well-trained in Reason's Decision-Making ways, Ego attacks do not throw you off course. When a difficult team situation happens, you immediately stop for a **moment of Reason**. You refocus on oneness, rise above the battleground, and remember to live your Work Agreements in your classroom.

To train your mind simply means practicing your team's Work Agreements, which represent your psychological goals, as often as possible, especially during difficult team situations.

Unified Circle of Right-Minded Thinking

When your team discusses and agrees on your psychological goals – your consciously chosen set of attitudes and behaviors as described in your Work Agreements – you have created your team's collective thought system.

By uniting with each other in this way and openly committing to one another through your Work Agreements, you are renouncing Ego in yourself and your teammates and collectively committing to train your minds to follow Reason.

This process of creating team Work Agreements is your undivided declaration of interdependence. Your assertion is saying,

> *We hold these mindful truths to be self-evident that all minds are created equal, and whosoever believes that will have everlasting freedom to choose Right-Minded Teamwork.*

Your declaration plus your daily acts of living your team Work Agreements ***is your return*** to the forgiving Unified Circle of Right-Minded Thinking.

Work Agreements

A Work Agreement is a collective promise made by teammates to transform non-productive, adversarial behavior into collaborative teamwork behavior. Work Agreements are a key tool for teammates and teams who aspire to do no harm and work as one.

Work Agreements are not flimsy ground rules. They are emotionally mature work performance commitments. Work Agreements announce your dedication to oneness and demonstrate your inner belief that "none of us is as smart as all of us."

Your team's collective Work Agreements also define your team's psychological goals and thought system. They ensure you conduct your day-to-day work from within your team's Unified Circle of Right-Minded Thinking.

To learn more about the power of Work Agreements and how to use them to transform your team, go to RightMindedTeamwork.com or your favorite book retailer, and pick up your copy of **How to Facilitate Team Work Agreements**: *A Practical, 10-Step Process for Building a Right-Minded Team That Works as One.*

About the Author

The idea of "developing people and teams that work" began as a company statement for organizational consulting firm Lord & Hogan LLC, founded in 1990. Leveraging his personable but results-oriented consulting style, founder **Dan Hogan** devoted his career to transforming dysfunctional work relationships into positive, supportive bonds.

But throughout his 40-year career, something shifted.

Through his work as an organizational development coach, performance consultant, and Certified Master Facilitator, the mission of Lord & Hogan also became Dan's own.

Better Work Relationships = Stronger, More Productive Teams

As a consultant and facilitator, Dan advocated for the individuals and managed teams he served. He emphasized the equal importance of strong team member relationships and solid business systems and processes to overall business success. His efforts spoke for themselves as his clients began to notice results.

With Dan's guidance, teams were more productive almost overnight. There were fewer day-to-day interpersonal issues. Project management efforts were finally back on track. Teams were achieving their goals.

After being stuck for so long, these teams were moving forward... smoothly. As one client said, "Dan has the unique ability to hear the confusion and bring clarity. He has helped me, our team, and our organization to move to the next level."

The Right-Minded Teamwork Model: A Legacy

Not only did Dan's efforts deliver consistent, powerful results (gaining him many long-term clients over the years) at a higher level, but his work also positively impacted the practice of behavioral change management.

Over the course of his career, Dan refined his ideas along with the help of his clients and the teams he served. Eventually, he created his own proprietary tools, processes, and strategies. Of all his models and creations, Dan's most significant accomplishment has been the development of his Right-Minded Teamwork model, which perfectly assembles all his tools and processes into a single, streamlined approach.

At its core, Right-Minded Teamwork (RMT) is a continuous improvement loop for small and large groups; it has been proven to work with teams of all sizes. No matter what team challenges or interpersonal issues are happening, RMT has the power to correct them.

By first bringing the team together under a unified set of goals, and then providing tools for teams to explore, understand, and work through their underlying concerns, Right-Minded Teamwork provides teams with the opportunity to address unproductive behaviors in a safe, non-condemning way. Focusing on acceptance, forgiveness, and self-adjustment among teammates, Right-Minded Teamwork directly addresses and resolves the root cause of even the most difficult teamwork situations.

After directly serving over 500 teams in seven countries and creating lasting tools and resources that will go on to support countless additional teams, leaders, and facilitators on every continent, Dan Hogan has left a legacy to be proud of. No longer an active facilitator, Dan has transformed his ideas and contributions into powerful, effective, team-building tools available online, providing team facilitators and team leaders around the globe access to Right-Minded Teamwork.

www.ingramcontent.com/pod-product-compliance
Lightning Source LLC
Chambersburg PA
CBHW072015110526
44592CB00012B/1322